# Steelers
## *Triviology*

Christopher Walsh

TRIUMPH
BOOKS

Years in the making, this one's for Clint.

---

*"I believe the game is designed to reward the ones who hit the hardest. If you can't take it, you shouldn't play."*
—Jack Lambert

---

Library of Congress Cataloging-in-Publication Data

Walsh, Christopher J., 1968–
  Steelers triviology / by Christopher Walsh.
      p. cm.
   ISBN 978-1-60078-621-1
 1. Pittsburgh Steelers (Football team)—Miscellanea. I. Title.
   GV959.P57W35 2011
   796.332'640974886—dc22

                        2011013346

This book is available in quantity at special discounts for your group or organization. For further information, contact:

  Triumph Books LLC
  814 North Franklin Street
  Chicago, Illinois 60610
  (800) 888-4741
  Fax (312) 337-1807
  www.triumphbooks.com

Printed in U.S.A.
ISBN: 978-1-60078-621-1
Design by Patricia Frey
Photos courtesy of AP Images except where otherwise noted.

# Contents

## One

# The Basics

Jim O'Brien told the following story in his book, *Doing it Right.*

One day during the offseason, Art Rooney was having dinner with sportscaster Curt Gowdy and their wives when the founder of the Pittsburgh Steelers learned that Ralph Giampaolo, a longtime member of the Three Rivers Stadium grounds crew, was also there at his dog track in Palm Beach.

Rooney invited Giampaolo up his private box to join them.

"I'll never forget the way he introduced me," Giampaolo recalled. "'This is Ralph Giampaolo, a member of our organization.' Not a member of our ground crew. Not some rinky-dink bum, but a member of our organization. As far as Gowdy knew, I was vice-president of the team. Mr. Rooney made me feel 10 feet tall."

Although Rooney died in 1988, there are still daily reminders of his influence and impact on the organization, including portraits, a statue outside of Heinz Field, and his cigars—which some people swear they can still smell.

When the Steelers recently celebrated their 75th anniversary, a special collection of items was put on display in the Coca-Cola Great Hall at Heinz Field, including throwback jerseys, Super Bowl footballs, and personal mementos of the Steelers.

At its heart though, was a glass case that held an ashtray with three spent matches and an unused vintage cigar. The name on the cigar box read *Braces*, an El Presidente brand imported from Honduras. And although there were various informative descriptions about who the items had belonged to and what the man was about, only three letters were needed at the front of the case to identify their significance: AJR.

Arthur Joseph Rooney.

Art Rooney sits behind his desk, enjoying one of his trademark cigars.
*(Getty Images)*

1. What's the origin of the Steelers' logo?
2. What are the three "stars" on the logo and what do the colors represent?
3. What color were the helmets when the logo was first used?
4. Who put the logo on only the right side of the helmet?
5. Why is it only on one side?
6. How much did Art Rooney pay to start the franchise in 1933?
7. According to Pittsburgh lore, how did he come up with the money?
8. In 2008, what did *Forbes* estimate the franchise to be worth?
9. True or false? The Rooney family has always owned the franchise.
10. True or false? In its early days the team played in places like Latrobe, Louisville, New Orleans, and Youngstown to avoid competing with baseball and college football?
11. Which number is bigger: the number of wins during the 1930s, or the number of head coaches?
12. True or false? The Steelers are the oldest franchise in the American Football Conference.
13. Who was considered the NFL's first big-money player?
14. How much was his contract with Pittsburgh worth?
15. What did he delay to sign the contract?
16. What prominent position did he go on to achieve?
17. Who was the last Steelers coach to not have a winning record?
18. Which popular college coach turned down the Steelers' offer to become head coach in 1969?
19. During its first 40 years, how many winning seasons did the franchise have?
20. Who came up with the idea of the Terrible Towel?
21. Who or what became the Steelers' official mascot in 2007?

22. True or false? Since the 1970 merger of the National and American Football Leagues, the Pittsburgh Steelers own the best regular-season record in the NFL.

23. Through the 2010 season, the Steelers had 577 total wins, the fourth most in NFL history. Name the three teams ahead of them.

24. Name the only team to have a better regular-season record in the free-agency era (since 1983).

25. How many head coaches have the Steelers had since 1969?

26. True or false? Mike Tomlin became the youngest head coach in NFL history to both coach in and win a Super Bowl when he led the Steelers to a 27–23 victory over the Arizona Cardinals in Super Bowl XLIII.

27. True or false? Only Bill Cowher was faster in winning a Super Bowl after becoming the head coach of the Steelers.

## Answers

1. It was the logo of the U.S. Steel Corporation (now known as USX Corporation), and later used by the American Iron and Steel Institute (AISI) to represent the whole industry. It was adopted by the Steelers in 1962.

2. The three "stars" are actually hypercycloids, and the colors represent the materials used to make steel: yellow for coal, orange for ore, and blue for steel scrap.

3. Yellow

4. Equipment manager Jack Hart.

5. The logo was only used on the right side because the organization wanted to test them out before making a final decision. When the 1962 Steelers finished 9–5 for its best finish to date, they kept them and further marked the occasion by changing the helmets from yellow to black.

6. $2,500

7. A big day at the racetrack.

8. $1 billion

9. False. Art Rooney sold it in 1940, only to reacquire it with a partner a year later.

10. According to The Football Encyclopedia, by David Neft, Richard Cohen, and Rick Korch (1994), it's true.

11. Pittsburgh had 22 wins in the 1930s, compared to five head coaches.

12. True

13. Byron "Whizzer" White

14. $15,800

15. His Rhodes scholarship.

16. Byron "Whizzer" White served 31 years as justice of the United States Supreme Court before retiring in 1993.

17. Bill Austin was 11–28–3 from 1966–68.

18. Joe Paterno

19. Nine

20. Myron Cope

21. Steely McBeam

22. True. Through the 2010 season the Steelers were 384–246–2, for a .612 winning percentage. The teams closest to them were the Miami Dolphins (379–251–2, .600) and Dallas Cowboys (373–259–0, .592).

23. The Chicago Bears (719), Green Bay Packers (690), and New York Giants (656).

24. The New England Patriots are 185–103–0 (.644) since 1993, while the Steelers are 181–106–1 (.630).

25. Three

26. True

27. False. Tomlin did it in his second year, making him the fastest to win a Super Bowl title in Steelers history.

*Two*

# League History

It all goes back to the 1860s and the campuses of two rival Ivy League schools, when Rutgers and Princeton decided to a play each other in a new sport that was a hybrid of soccer and rugby, but looked more like an organized riot. On November 6, 1869, they met using modified London Football Association rules and Rutgers won 6–4, despite one of its professors pointing his umbrella at participants and yelling, "You will come to no Christian end." There were roughly 100 people in attendance.

From there, the game quickly began to evolve, with Walter Camp, considered the father of American football, setting down rules in 1876 and continued to revise them until his death in 1925. His numerous innovations included one side potentially having undisputed possession of the ball until it gave it up or scored, the number of players on the field for each team reduced from 15 to 11, and the creation of the quarterback and center positions, in addition to the forward pass.

While football became a major attraction of local athletic clubs, with the Allegheny Athletic Association and Pittsburgh Athletic Club credited with having the first professionals, the first attempt at a pro league was made in 1902 when baseball's Philadelphia Athletics (managed by Connie Mack) and Philadelphia Phillies created pro football teams, joining the Pittsburgh Stars.

After years of unsettled confusion—with salaries rising, players jumping from team to team, and college athletes being used while still in school—an organizational meeting was held in 1920 at the Jordan and Humpmobile auto showroom in Canton, Ohio, to begin drawing up plans for a centralized league with one set of rules, the American Professional Football Conference. Two years later, the APFA changed its name to the National Football League.

The rest, as they say, is history.

1.  What law change benefitted both the Pirates (now Steelers) and Eagles when they entered the NFL?
2.  Who came up with the idea to hold an annual draft of college players, with teams selecting in inverse order?
3.  When his team entered the league, owner Bert Bell doubled in what capacity for the Philadelphia Eagles?
4.  In 1936, a rival league was formed, the second to call itself the American Football League. Which team won its championship?
5.  In 1940, a rival league was formed, the third to call itself the American Football League. Which team won its championship?
6.  Who was the first NFL commissioner?
7.  How many NFL players died fighting in World War II?

8. Who was named commissioner in 1946, and where did he move the league offices?

9. What eventually ended his reign?

10. In 1948, what piece of equipment was banned, and what did officials replace with whistles?

11. When the NFL and All-American Football Conference announced a merger agreement, which three teams were added to the NFL in 1950?

12. What league-changing rule became permanent in 1950?

13. What association was founded in 1956?

14. True or false? The highest scoring season in league history was 1965.

15. Who appeared in the first Super Bowl ad that really became a part of pop culture?

16. After an 11-week trial in 1986, what did the U.S. District Court in New York award the United States Football League in its $1.7 billion antitrust suit against the NFL?

17. Which Steelers were named to the NFL's All-Decade Team in the 1960s?

18. Which Steelers were named to the NFL's All-Decade Team in the 1970s?

19. Which Steelers were named to the NFL's All-Decade Team in the 1980s?

20. Which Steelers were named to the NFL's All-Decade Team in the 1990s?

21. Which Steelers were named to the NFL's All-Decade Team in the 2000s?

## Answers

1. A change in Pennsylvania law permitted football games to be played on Sundays.
2. Bert Bell of the Philadelphia Eagles.
3. In addition to owner, Bert Bell was also the Eagles' coach, general manager, publicity director, and ticket director.
4. The Boston Shamrocks.
5. The Columbus Bullies.
6. Elmer Layden
7. 21
8. Steelers co-owner Bert Bell, who moved the league offices to Philadelphia.
9. He died of a massive heart attack while watching the Eagles and Steelers play in Philadelphia on October 11, 1959.
10. Plastic helmets and whistles replaced horns.
11. Baltimore, Cleveland, and San Francisco.
12. The free-substitution rule.
13. The NFL Players Association.
14. False, it was actually 1948 when NFL teams averaged 23.2 points per game and three of the 10 teams averaged more than 30. The 1965 season saw the second-most scoring, 23.1
15. Farrah Fawcett lathering Noxzema shaving cream on Joe Namath's face in 1973.
16. $1
17. No one.
18. Lynn Swann, Joe Greene, Jack Ham, Terry Bradshaw, Franco Harris, Mike Webster, L.C. Greenwood, Jack Lambert, and coach Chuck Noll.
19. Mel Blount, Mike Webster, Jack Lambert, Gary Anderson, and Chuck Noll.
20. Kevin Greene, Rod Woodson, Dermontti Dawson, Hardy Nickerson, Levon Kirkland, Carnell Lake, and Gary Anderson.
21. Alan Faneca, Joey Porter, and Troy Polamalu.

*Three*

# Famous Firsts

In 1933, when President Franklin D. Roosevelt was in the midst of trying to pull the country out of the Great Depression, the struggling National Football League was ready to make some changes.

After Dutch Clark of the Portsmouth Spartans led the league in field goals with three, and only six were attempted, the goalposts were moved up to the goal line. Passing was allowed from anywhere behind the line of scrimmage instead of at least five years back, and the precursor to hash marks was created when the spot of the ball was moved 10 yards in from the sideline for the subsequent snap after any play ending within five yards of the out-of-bounds line.

But it was also when the eight-team league added two eventual strong pillars with Pittsburgh and Philadelphia, which were owned by Art Rooney and Bert Bell, respectively. Both certainly had their hands full the first few years, as did the other pioneers.

The Cincinnati Reds also joined the league in 1933, after the Staten Island Stapletons folded, but they only lasted a year. Portsmouth moved to Detroit in 1934, the Boston Braves became the Washington Redskins in 1937, the same year the Cleveland Rams came into the fold.

While the Steelers only won 22 games during their first seven seasons, Rooney and Bell ended up having crucial secondary roles, frequently acting as mediators and buffers between outspoken and frequently stubborn owners George Halas of the Chicago Bears and George Preston Marshall of the Braves/Redskins.

Without them, the league might have developed very differently, or possibly failed to survive.

1. What day is considered the franchise's birthday?
2. How old was Art Rooney when he founded the Pirates?
3. True or false? Rooney had been running a semipro team for years.
4. Who was the first coach?
5. Which team was the first opponent?
6. Where was the game played?
7. What was the estimated attendance?
8. Who scored the first points in a franchise game and how?
9. Who scored the first points in franchise history and how?
10. Who scored the first touchdown in franchise history and how?
11. Who scored the first offensive touchdown and how?
12. Against which team was the first victory? (Bonus: Name the score.)
13. During the first season, what was Mose Kelsch's claim to fame?
14. The 1933 season was the first featuring an NFL championship game. Which team won?
15. What division did the Pirates first play in?
16. True or false? It was the first year the NFL had divisions.
17. How many teams did the NFL have in 1933?

18. How many games did Pittsburgh win its first season?
19. True or false? The Pirates had the league's worst record that year.
20. True or false? They scored the fewest points in the league.
21. True or false? They gave up the most points.
22. In 1934, who was the first replacement at head coach?
23. What season was the first in which Pittsburgh didn't finish last in its division?
24. Who was the first Steelers player to lead the league in rushing? (Bonus: Name the year and number of yards.)
25. True or false? The franchise won its last game as the Pirates.
26. True or false? The franchise won its first game as the Steelers.
27. What year did the franchise record its first winning season?
28. When did it qualify for the playoffs for the first time?
29. Who was the first Steelers player to win the league's most valuable player award?
30. True or false? Chuck Noll won his first game coaching the Steelers.
31. Which was not true of Bill Cowher's first season?
    a. The Steelers won his first game.
    b. The Steelers won the division.
    c. The Steelers were the AFC's top-seeded playoff team.
    d. The Steelers won the Super Bowl.
    e. All are true.

**Answers**

1. July 8, 1933
2. 32
3. True
4. Jap Douds
5. The New York Giants, who won 23–2.
6. Forbes Field
7. 20,000
8. Ken Strong of the Giants scored on a 33-yard interception return and then kicked the extra point.
9. Lineman Cap Oehler blocked a punt through the end zone for a safety.
10. Marty Kottler scored the first touchdown in franchise history on a 99-yard interception return against the Chicago Cardinals.

Coach Bill Cowher
fired up during a
1992 win over the
Houston Oilers.

11. End Paul Moss scored the first offensive touchdown in franchise history on a 10-yard reception from Bill Tanguay against the Chicago Cardinals.

12. In their second game the Pirates defeated the Chicago Cardinals 14–13.

13. The 37-year-old kicker made a last-second field goal to tie the Brooklyn Dodgers 3–3.

14. The Chicago Bears beat the New York Giants 23–21.

15. Eastern Division

16. True

17. 10

18. Three. The Pirates went 3–6–2.

19. False, the Chicago Cardinals were 1–9–1.

20. False, the Cincinnati Reds, which somehow managed to win three games as well, only scored 38.

21. True, 208. Philadelphia yielded the second-most points with 158.

22. Luby DiMelio

23. 1935. It went 4–8–0 to finish third in the Eastern Division.

24. Byron "Whizzer" White, with 567 rushing yards on 152 carries in 1938.

25. False, the Pirates lost at Philadelphia, 7–0.

26. False. The Steelers tied the Chicago Cardinals, 7–7.

27. 1942, the Steelers went 7–4.

28. 1947. The Steelers lost to Philadelphia 21–0 in the Eastern Division playoff.

29. Bill Dudley in 1946.

30. True. In 1969, the Steelers opened with a 16–13 victory against the Detroit Lions—and then lost every game the rest of the season to finish 1–13.

31. d. The Steelers did everything but win the Super Bowl, losing to Buffalo in the divisional playoffs.

# Four

# Stadiums

In 1933, when Art Rooney founded the Pittsburgh Pirates, he obviously needed a place to host games, and settled on the stadium that served as home to the baseball team with the same name.

Forbes Field was built in 1909 on seven acres of land near the Carnegie Library of Pittsburgh adjacent to Schenley Park for $1 million—although some estimates have the cost as actually twice that amount. Instead of the popular wooden ballparks of the time it featured a three-tiered structure built out of steel and concrete, the first of its kind. The only ballpark ever designed by civil engineer Charles Willford Leavitt Jr., construction only took 122 days and its light green steelwork was contrasted by the red slate of the roof.

In 1970, the Cubs and Pirates closed the 62-year old stadium with Pittsburgh winning 4–1, and along with the Steelers, moved into Three Rivers Stadium. After two fires, abandoned Forbes Field was torn down and cleared for use by the University of Pittsburgh, where home plate remains on display in the lobby floor of Posvar Hall. A sidewalk plaque marks where Bill Mazeroski's famous home run to end the 1960 World Series cleared the wall.

1. Who was Forbes Field named after?
2. What football team first called Forbes Field home?
3. How many undefeated seasons did that team enjoy when it called Forbes Field home? (Bonus: Name the years.)
4. Which teams played in the first football game at Forbes Field? (Bonus: Name the score.)
5. What first occurred at Forbes Field on October 8, 1921?
6. When the Pittsburgh Pirates lost their first regular-season game on September 20, 1933, who wrote, "The Giants won. Our team looks terrible. The fans didn't get their money's worth."?
7. Who did the Steelers score nine touchdowns against at Forbes Field on November 30, 1952? (Bonus: Name the final score.)
8. Under what conditions was that game played?
9. How did the hometown fans react?
10. Why did the Steelers start playing games at Pitt Stadium in 1958?
11. True or false? With Pitt splitting its home games between Forbes Field and Pitt Stadium from 1958 to 1963, fans were able to purchase season-ticket packages for one site if they wanted.
12. When did the Steelers play their last game at Forbes Field?
13. True or false? The Steelers won.
14. True or false? The Steelers won their last game at Pitt Stadium? (Bonus: Name the opponent.)
15. How much did Three Rivers Stadium cost to build?
16. How much did the land cost?
17. What was it named after?
18. What three other stadiums—two outdoor and one indoor—did it resemble? (Bonus: Name the nickname given to all four.)

19. Which team did the Steelers play in their first regular-season game at Three Rivers Stadium and what was the result?
20. True or false? The 1970–72 seasons were the only ones in which the Steelers didn't sell out every home game at Three Rivers Stadium.
21. True or false? The Steelers had 100 or more victories than losses at Three Rivers Stadium.
22. Out of 18 playoffs games at Three Rivers Stadium how many did the Steelers lose?
23. What two other football teams called Three Rivers Stadium home?
24. Which team did Pittsburgh play in the final game at Three Rivers Stadium? (Bonus: Name the score.)
25. True or false? The stadium still stands.
26. A sequence from what music documentary about a rock band was filmed at Three Rivers Stadium?
27. How far away from Three Rivers Stadium was Heinz Field constructed?
28. When did Heinz Field open?
29. What's the address?
30. How much did it cost?
31. True or false? The H.J. Heinz Company owns the stadium.
32. How much steel was used to build it?
33. What was the first event held at Heinz Field?
34. True or false? The Steelers lost their first game there during the preseason against Detroit.
35. What was the attendance?
36. Who won the first football game at Heinz Field?
37. Who scored the first touchdown in the stadium?
38. Why was the Steelers' first home game at Heinz Field delayed?
39. Which team was scheduled to be the first regular-season opponent at Heinz Field and which team did it end up being? (Bonus: Name the winning team and score.)

40. Who scored the first NFL points at Heinz Field?
41. Who scored the first NFL touchdown?
42. True or false? Since 1970, the Steelers have the best home record in the NFL.

## Answers

1. Forbes Field was named in honor of General John Forbes, who captured Fort Duquesne from the French in 1758 and rebuilt it as Fort Pitt.
2. The University of Pittsburgh
3. Five: 1910, 1915, 1916, 1917, and 1918.
4. On October 16, 1909, Pitt defeated Bucknell University 18–6.
5. West Virginia at Pitt was the first live radio broadcast of a college football game in the United States.
6. Art Rooney
7. The New York Giants, 63–7.
8. Snowy
9. Many of the 15,140 spectators rushed the field and tried to tear down the goalposts.
10. The University of Pittsburgh acquired Forbes Field for $2 million and Pitt Stadium was larger.
11. True
12. December 1, 1963
13. False, they tied the Philadelphia Eagles 20–20.
14. False, they lost to the New York Giants 21–17. Actually, they lost their last six games there in 1969 during the 1–13 season.
15. $35 million.
16. $20 million (thus, the entire project cost roughly $55 million).
17. The confluence of the Allegheny and Monongahela Rivers, which form the Ohio River.
18. Riverfront Stadium, Busch Memorial Stadium, and the Houston Astrodome were also known as "cookie-cutter" stadiums.
19. The Steelers lost to the Houston Oilers 19–7.
20. True
21. True, the Steelers were 182–72 at Three Rivers Stadium.
22. Five
23. The Pittsburgh Maulers of the United States Football League and the University of Pittsburgh.
24. On December 16, 2000, the Steelers beat the Washington Redskins, 24–3.
25. False. It was imploded in 2001.
26. Led Zeppelin's *The Song Remains the Same*.
27. At its closest point 80 feet
28. 2001
29. 100 Art Rooney Avenue, Pittsburgh, Pennsylvania 15212
30. $281 million

31. False, the Sports & Exhibition Authority of Pittsburgh and Allegheny County owns it. Heinz is paying $57 million through 2021 for the naming rights.
32. 12,000 tons
33. An 'N Sync concert on August 18, 2001.
34. False. The Steelers beat the Lions 20–7.
35. 57,829
36. Pitt beat East Tennessee State 31–0.
37. Quarterback David Priestley on an 85-yard run.
38. The September 11, 2001 terrorist attacks.
39. The game against the Cleveland Browns was moved to the end of the regular season, making the Cincinnati Bengals the Steelers' first opponent on October 7, 2001. The Steelers won 16–7.
40. Kicker Kris Brown on a 26-yard field goal
41. Quarterback Kordell Strewart on an 8-yard run.
42. True, through the 2010 season the Steelers were 227–88–1 (.720) at home since 1970, and are 58–21–1 at Heinz Field.

# Five

# Nicknames

For those of you paying close attention, you're already aware that the original nickname of the Pittsburgh Steelers was Pirates.

What's in a nickname? Well, even though it was fairly common at the time for NFL teams to take the same name as the city's Major League Baseball squad, the franchise opted for its own identity and adopted Steelers in 1940.

However, in a further break from tradition, both the Pirates and later the NHL's Pittsburgh Penguins ended up following the Steelers instead of the other way around.

Before the baseball team was known as the Pirates, it was called the Alleghenys, in reference to the city that would be annexed by Pittsburgh in 1907. While the struggling franchise was already in the National League, in 1890 it made a claim on second basemen Lou Bierbauer after the Philadelphia Athletics of the American Association failed to put him on its reserve list. When an American Association official described the move as "piratical," the franchise decided to have fun with it by changing the nickname.

While the football team originally wore gold helmets and black jerseys, the baseball team switched from red, white, and blue to the same color scheme as the Steelers. Incidentally, it's also featured in the city's flag. The black and gold was also eventually worn by the Penguins, the Pittsburgh Power of the Arena Football League and even the Pittsburgh Passion of the Independent Women's Football League.

"Mean" Joe Greene appears along with child actor Tommy Okon in this still photo from the famous 1979 Coca-Cola commercial.

Try to come up with the popular nicknames for the following:

1.  Jerome Bettis
2.  Will Blackwell
3.  Terry Bradshaw
4.  Bill Cowher
5.  Dermontti Dawson
6.  James Farrior
7.  Barry Foster
8.  Chris Fuamatu-Ma'afala
9.  Fans of Ron Gerela
10. Joe Gilliam
11. L.C. Greenwood
12. Joe Greene
13. Jack Ham
14. Casey Hampton
15. Fans of Franco Harris
16. Arnold Harrison
17. James Harrison
18. Merril Hoge
19. Evander Hood
20. Eddie Holmes
21. Norm Johnson
22. Brett Keisel
23. Levon Kirkland
24. Chris Kemoeatu
25. Jack Lambert
26. Bobby Layne

27. Tim Lester
28. Louis Lipps
29. Greg Lloyd
30. Tommy Maddox
31. Johnny McNally
32. Rashard Mendenhall
33. Heath Miller
34. Mewelde Moore
35. Byron Morris
36. Mike Mularkey
37. Chuck Noll
38. Neil O'Donnell
39. Raymond Parker
40. Willie Parker
41. Troy Polamalu
42. Jerry Porter
43. Jeff Reed
44. Ben Roethlisberger
45. Art Rooney
46. Bill Shakespeare
47. Billy Ray Smith
48. Max Starks
49. Kordell Stewart
50. Hugh Taylor
51. Hines Ward
52. Mike Webster

53. Byron White
54. Dwight White
55. Keith Willis

56. LaMarr Woodley
57. Rod Woodson
58. Amos Zereoue

**Answers**

1. The Bus
2. Hubba Bubba
3. Blonde Bomber
4. The Jaw
5. Ned Flanders
6. Potsie
7. Bananas
8. Fu
9. Gerela's Gorillas
10. Jefferson Street Joe
11. Hollywood Bags
12. Mean or Mean Joe
13. *Dobre Shunka*, which means "good ham" in Polish or Slovak.
14. Big Snack
15. Franco's Italian Army
16. Smelly
17. Silverback or Deebo
18. Hogie
19. Ziggy
20. Fats or Arrowhead
21. Mr. Automatic
22. Diesel
23. Big Kirk
24. Wedge or Juicy
25. Dracula
26. Gadabout Gladiator
27. The Bus Driver
28. Hot Lips
29. Just Plain Nasty
30. Tommy Gun or Touchdown Tommy
31. Blood
32. Delicious
33. Big Money
34. Waltzing Mewelde
35. Bam
36. Inspector Gadget
37. Emporer Chaz
38. Sup
39. Buddy
40. Fast Willie
41. Tasmanian Devil or Taz
42. Peezy
43. Creech or Hayseed
44. Big Ben
45. The Chief
46. The Bard of Staten Island
47. The Rabbit
48. The Undertaker
49. Slash
50. Bones
51. Woedee (which is a derivative of "Wardy")
52. Iron Mike or Papa Smurf
53. Whizzer
54. Mad Dog
55. Skippy
56. The Wood
57. Hot Rod
58. Famous Amos

## Six

# Jersey Numbers

What's in a number? Sometimes a lot. When *Sports Illustrated* put together its list of the best NFL players by jersey numbers, eight Pittsburgh Steelers were named, trailing only the Chicago Bears (nine).

The eight selected were: No. 26: Rod Woodson; No. 36: Jerome Bettis; No. 43: Troy Polamalu; No. 47: Mel Blount; No. 58: Jack Lambert; No. 59: Jack Ham; No. 68: L.C. Greenwood; and No. 91: Kevin Greene.

Interestingly, most of those are not considered to be among the almost sacred numbers by Steelers fans (we'll get to that in a moment).

Unless specified, the following questions are regarding jersey numbers through the 2009 season.

1. Who is the only Steelers player to have his number retired, and what was it?
2. What four numbers will almost certainly be never worn again by a Pittsburgh Steeler?
3. Who last wore them?
4. Until 2010, who was the only player to wear No. 26 after Rod Woodson?
5. Who has worn No. 36 since Jerome Bettis?
6. True or false? No one has worn No. 47 since Mel Blount.
7. What number did Dwayne Woodruff wear?
8. Name anyone who has worn No. 68 since L.C. Greenwood.
9. Whose number has also not been issued since he retired in 1990? (Bonus: What is the number?)
10. Which number did that player also briefly wear?
11. Who was the only player in franchise history to wear No. 00?
12. Which two players wore No. 0?
13. Which number hasn't been given out since 1954?
14. Who's the only player since 1967 to wear No. 6?
15. What number did Jack Kemp wear during his lone season with Pittsburgh?
16. Which number had a 61-year absence between players?
17. What number did Tony Dungy wear?
18. What number wasn't given out until 1987? (Bonus: Name who wore it.)
19. What number did John Goodman (not the actor) wear?
20. What number did kicker Gary Anderson wear?

Mike Webster at Three
Rivers Stadium in December
1988. *(Getty Images)*

## Answers

1. Ernie Stautner, No. 70
2. Numbers 12, 32, 58, and 75.
3. Terry Bradshaw, Franco Harris, Jack Lambert, and Joe Greene.
4. Deshea Townsend
5. No one
6. False. Actually, five players have: Steve Morse, Cameron Riley, Bruce Jones, Scott Shields, and Ron Stanley.
7. No. 49
8. Jeff Lucas, Lorenzo Freeman, Mike Withycombe, Lonnie Palelei, Brenden Stai, Shar Pourdanesh, Keydrick Vincent, and Chris Kemoeatu.
9. No. 52, Mike Webster.
10. No. 53
11. Johnny Clement (1946–48)
12. Jack Collins (1952) and Johnny Clement (1946–48).
13. No. 13, which was worn by Bull Mackrides.
14. Bubby Brister
15. No. 7
16. No. 8, which was in disuse between Everett Fisher in 1940 and Tommy Maddox in 2001.
17. No. 21
18. No. 99, worn by Michael Minter.
19. No. 95
20. No. 1

*Seven*

# Records

In some NFL media guides the section on individual records begins with a bit of a disclaimer that should always be taken into consideration when it comes to season and career statistics.

In 1960, the regular season lasted just 12 games, which was probably a good thing for Steelers fans, who were enduring yet another non-playoff season with a 5–6–1 record under head coach Buddy Parker.

With the addition of the expansion Minnesota Vikings in 1961, the regular season was increased to 14 games, which it maintained through 1977. In 1978, with some fans complaining about having to pay for several preseason games in addition to the regular season as part of their season-ticket packages, the league added two more games to the schedule plus more wild-card entries for the playoffs so that more teams would still be in contention for the postseason during the final weeks of the season.

Just something to keep in mind when looking over the numbers.

1. Who holds the team record for 100-yard rushing games?
2. Who had the most passes intercepted?
3. Who holds the team record in forced fumbles?
4. Who played the most seasons and games for the Steelers and how many of each did he have?
5. The longest reception in Steelers in history is 90 yards. Who did it first?
6. Who threw the pass?
7. Who were the other two players to have a 90-yard reception?
8. Who has the longest run in Steelers history?
9. True or false? The Steelers hold the record for fewest touchdown passes in a season with zero.
10. How many interceptions and turnovers did the Steelers have against Philadelphia on December 12, 1965, to set NFL records in both categories?
11. Which Steelers punter holds the NFL record for having six punts blocked in a single season?
12. Who kicked the longest punt in team history?
13. Who holds the NFL record for punt-return yards by a rookie?
14. How many consecutive games did Ben Roethlisberger win at the start of his career, to set an NFL record?
15. Who had the previous record for wins to start an NFL career? (Hint: He played for the Steelers.)
16. How many times did Ben Roethlisberger pass for more than 300 yards in 2009, to set a team record? (Bonus: Name who previously held the record.)

17. When he retired in 1962 after 15 seasons, which NFL career records did Bobby Layne hold?
    a. Passes attempted
    b. Passes completed
    c. Passing yards gained
    d. Passing touchdowns
    e. All of the above
    f. None of the above
18. What's the franchise record for most Pro Bowl selections in a single year?
19. Name them.
20. Who tied Paul Brown for the most consecutive playoff appearances to start a head coaching career in the NFL, with six?
21. What did the Steelers become the first team in AFC history to do, in 2004?
22. What three NFC teams had already done that?
23. What epic NFL-record winning streak did Pittsburgh end in 2004?

*Name the individual team record holders in the following categories (Bonus: List the numbers too).*
24. Career rushing yards
25. Career passing yards
26. Career passing touchdowns
27. Career receptions
28. Career receiving yards
29. Career receiving touchdowns
30. Career interceptions
31. Career interceptions for a touchdown
32. Career punting average
33. Career punt-return average
34. Career kick-return average
35. Career field goals

36. Career touchdowns
37. Career points
38. Season rushing yards
39. Season passing yards
40. Season passing touchdowns
41. Season receptions
42. Season receiving yards
43. Season interceptions
44. Season punting average
45. Season punt-return average
46. Season kick-return average
47. Season field goals
48. Season touchdowns
49. Season points
50. Game rushing yards
51. Game passing yards
52. Game passing touchdowns
53. Game receptions
54. Game receiving yards
55. Game interceptions
56. Game field goals
57. Game touchdowns
58. Game points
59. Career sacks
60. Career fumble recoveries
61. Which opposing player had the best rushing performance against the Steelers?
62. Which opposing player had the best passing performance against the Steelers?
63. Which opposing player had the best receiving performance against the Steelers?

**Answers**

1. Jerome Bettis, with 50.
2. Terry Bradshaw, with 210.
3. Greg Lloyd, 36.
4. Mike Webster has played the most seasons (15) and games (220).
5. Quarterback Mark Malone had a 90-yard reception against Seattle in 1981.
6. Quarterback Terry Bradshaw threw it.
7. Bubby Brister to Dwight Stone vs. Denver in 1990, and Kordell Stewart to Bobby Shaw vs. Baltimore in 2001.
8. Bobby Gage, 97 yards vs. the Chicago Bears in 1949.
9. True, the Steelers did it in 1945.
10. Nine and 12 respectively.
11. Harry "Three-Step" Newsome (1988).
12. Joe Geri, 82 yards vs. Green Bay on November 20, 1949.
13. Louis Lipps, 656, in 1984.
14. 15.
15. Mike Kruczek went 6–0 while filling in for injured Terry Bradshaw in 1976.
16. Five. Tommy Maddox (2003) and Neil O'Donnell (1995) had the previous record with four.
17. e. All of the above. Layne had the NFL career records for passes attempted (3,700), completed (1,814), passing yards (26,768), and passing touchdowns (196).
18. 11 in 1976.
19. Mel Blount, Terry Bradshaw, Glen Edwards, Joe Greene, L.C. Greenwood, Jack Ham, Franco Harris, Jack Lambert, Andy Russell, Lynn Swann, and Mike Wagner.
20. Bill Cowher
21. Win 15 games during a 16-game schedule.
22. The 1984 San Francisco 49ers, 1985 Chicago Bears, and 1998 Minnesota Vikings.
23. Pittsburgh snapped New England's 21-game winning streak.
24. Career rushing yards: Franco Harris, 11,950.
25. Career passing yards: Terry Bradshaw, 27,899.
26. Career passing touchdowns: Terry Bradshaw, 212.
27. Career receptions: Hines Ward, 954 (through 2010).
28. Career receiving yards: Hines Ward, 11,702 (through 2010).
29. Career receiving touchdowns: Hines Ward, 83 (through 2010).
30. Career interceptions: Mel Blount, 57.
31. Career interception returns for a touchdown: Rod Woodson, five.
32. Career punting average: Bobby Joe Green (19960-61), 45.7.
33. Career punt-return average: Bobby Gage (1949–50) 14.9

34. Career kick-return average: Lynn Chandnois (1950–56), 29.6.
35. Career field goals: Gary Anderson, 309
36. Career touchdowns: Franco Harris, 100
37. Career points: Gary Anderson, 1,343
38. Season rushing yards: Barry Foster (1992), 1,690.
39. Season passing yards: Ben Roethlisberger (2009), 4,328.
40. Season passing touchdowns: Ben Roethlisberger (2009), 32.
41. Season receptions: Hines Ward (2009), 112.
42. Season receiving yards: Yancy Thigpen (1997), 1,398.
43. Season interceptions: Mel Blount (1975), 11.
44. Season punting average: Bobby Joe Green (1961), 47.0.
45. Season punt-return average: Bobby Gage (1949), 16.0.
46. Season kick-return average: Lynn Chandnois (1952), 35.2.
47. Season field goals: Norm Johnson (1995), 34.
48. Season touchdowns: Willie Parker (2006), 16.
49. Season points: Norm Johnson (1995), 141
50. Game rushing yards: Willie Parker (December 7, 2006 vs. Cleveland), 223.
51. Game passing yards: Ben Roethlisberger (December 20, 2009), 503.
52. Game passing touchdowns: Ben Roethlisberger (November 5, 2007 vs. Baltimore), Mark Malone (September 8, 1985 vs. Indianapolis), and Terry Bradshaw (November 15, 1981 at Atlanta), five.
53. Game receptions: Courtney Hawkins (November 1, 1998 vs. Tennessee), 14.
54. Game receiving yards: Plaxico Burress (November 10, 2002 vs. Atlanta), 253.
55. Game interceptions: Jack Butler (December 13, 1953), four.
56. Game field goals: Jeff Reed (December 1, 2002 vs. Jacksonville), and Gary Anderson (December 23, 1988 vs. Denver), six.
57. Game touchdowns: Roy Jefferson (November 3, 1968 vs. Atlanta) and Ray Matthews (November 17, 1954 vs. Cleveland, four.
58. Game points: Roy Jefferson (November 3, 1968 vs. Atlanta) and Ray Matthews (November 17, 1954 vs. Cleveland, 24.
59. Career sacks: Jason Gildon, 77.
60. Career fumble recoveries: Ernie Stautner, 23.
61. Fred Taylor, 234 rushing yards on 30 carries and three touchdowns for Jacksonville on November 19, 2000.
62. Doug Williams, 30 of 52 attempts for 430 passing yards for Washington on September 11, 1988.
63. Qadry Ismail, six receptions for 258 yards and three touchdowns for Baltimore on December 12, 1999.

## *Eight*

# Quotes

The favorite football flick of most Steelers fans isn't *Any Given Sunday* or *The Longest Yard* (Even though Paul "Wrecking" Crewe was a former Steelers quarterback). Instead, it's a little-known, made-for-TV gem. In 1980, Robert Urich stared in *Fighting Back: The Rocky Bleier Story*, which told the story of the Steelers running back who, after making the team, was drafted and served in the U.S. Army during the Vietnam War. He was seriously injured there, but managed to come back and become a fan favorite.

Specifically, Bleier was drafted for duty after his rookie year and on August 20, 1969, his platoon was ambushed in a rice paddy near Chu Lai. He was struck by a bullet in his left thigh and, while down, a grenade exploded nearby, sending pieces of shrapnel into his right leg and foot. Bleier was told that he'd never walk again.

While recovering in a hospital in Tokyo, Bleier received a postcard from Art Rooney. "I was pleased he took the time," he later told *Sports Illustrated*. "The card said something like 'We're still behind you. Take care of yourself, and we'll see you when you get back.' That was nice." When he reported to training camp in 1970, Bleier couldn't walk without pain, had a noticeable limp, and was 30 pounds under his previous playing weight.

Bleier was waived twice and nearly quit football in 1973, but he continued to work and eventually not only reclaimed a spot on the roster but became a starter. He had a 1,000-yard rushing season in 1976 and he caught the decisive touchdown pass in Super Bowl XIII—one of his four rings.

"I'm a breathing example of what you can do if you want to," Bleier said.

As far as quotes go, you can't get much better than that. But let's try. Name who made the following statements.

1. "Chuck Noll is building one hell of a football team up in Pittsburgh. I look for the Steelers to be the team of the future. Just remember I said that."
2. "If I could start my life all over again, I would be a professional football player, and you damn well better believe I'd be a Pittsburgh Steeler."
3. "If that boy billionaire thinks he can shut me up, he should stick his head in a can of paint."
4. "It's like what they said about the raptor in *Jurassic Park*: one of us gets your attention, the other one gets you."
5. "Before you can win a game, you have to not lose it."
6. "Well, we've got a new team, a new coach, a new nickname, and new uniforms, but they look like the same old Pirates to me."
7. "From my perspective, you learn more in failure than you do in success."
8. "They say that when you're the champs, everybody will try to beat you. Well, I'm glad we're champs, so bring 'em on, bring 'em all on. If we die, we ain't gonna die running. It's gonna be a fight."

9. "With so many Super Bowl rings, maybe they'll all retire and go into the jewelry business."

10. "We consider our Super Bowl trophy an antique."

11. "It's time to plant some seeds. What that means is, hit them in the mouth. Ya know, plant some seeds. Show 'em what time it is."

12. "Going after the QB is like playing king of the mountain. When you get the QB, you're on top of the mountain."

13. "The harder we played, the behinder we got."

14. "To be honest, the fans pay our bills. They pay my bills. They pay for my house and everything else. That's the best feeling in the world to come out and see 60,000 people at a football game."

15. "We had a standing rule in my house: Nobody was allowed to mention the Steelers for two days after we lost. That's how much it bothered me."

16. "I want to bring back the pride and tradition long associated with the Pittsburgh Steelers, and more importantly, with the people of Pittsburgh."

17. "What's the worst thing that can happen to a quarterback? He loses his confidence."

18. "The Steelers drafted guys who were bigger, stronger, and faster than I, but they never found one who could take my job away from me."

19. "People are ranking us up there with the fabled Packers and Dolphins. It's nice to be fabled."

20. "Chuck and I hit it off the first day we met. We had an argument."

21. "We're a team of fighters. We don't quit. We believe in each other. We were going to fight all the way to the last second, which I think we did."

22. "On Saturday, there's a tarp there and I see everything is fine. On Sunday, I couldn't believe it. Here the field is frozen and they've got a hose out there and they're watering it down. I'm standing there watching them and they're telling me they're trying to melt the ice!"

23. "You come out hurting all over, and what didn't hurt, didn't work."

24. "I'll be glad to leave here. I feel like eating palm trees. I don't like this place. It's for people with arthritis. They come here to play golf and die"

25. "Dreith said I hit Sipe too hard. I hit him as hard as I could. Brian has a chance to go out of bounds and he decides not to. He knows I'm going to hit him. And I do. History."

26. "He had no teeth, and he was slobbering all over himself. I'm thinking, 'You can have your money back, just get me out of here. Let me go be an accountant.' I can't tell you how badly I wanted out of there."

27. "I'm not out there to pussyfoot or be your friend. I have a lot of friends around the league. But I don't know you when you're on the field. I play the game."

28. "Now that I'm here, I don't want to just be here, I want to be here for a long time."

29. "It's the high-character players. On paper you wouldn't say they'd win Super Bowls like [the Steelers] did, but if you don't have the chemistry, the talent and the help, with high-character people, you're not going to survive."

30. "I am very aggressive and very physical. On the field I guess I am just plain mean."

31. "Toughest [loss] I've ever had in my life."

32. "We're coming from everywhere. We play with 15 guys in the huddle. We have guys parachuting from airplanes, fans coming from out of the stands to help us go after people."

33. "Money talks and everything else walks."

34. "Wins and losses are black and white and it's pure, it's purity."

35. "Who is Joe Namath? This is a guy who, if he played in the league today, I'd probably just go hit him late and see what he did, just for the hell of it. Joe Namath can go to hell. He can kiss [my] ass."

36. "I'm no [expletive] relief quarterback. I don't mop up for anybody."

37. "You play your whole career for [a shot at] free agency."

38. "He has speed, soft hands, and grace."

39. "I hated putting on that purple uniform, and I hated that Raven bird. What really ticked me off is when we played Pittsburgh and our whole stadium seemed to be filled with Pittsburgh fans."

40. "My mentality is singular in that I want to be world champs each and every year, so that's what we work toward. I have a tough time acknowledging levels of success short of that."

41. "The only thing I want to see different is that there were a lot of Steelers fans there—which is great for the Steelers, but this is our home."

42. "Franco who?"

43. "Big men on blades of grass...the most violent team is going to win."

44. "We're a road team. We're the Pittsburgh Steelers. We have fans everywhere."

45. "This is Pittsburgh. If you don't win the Super Bowl, it's a bust. The guys in the 1970s created that mentality. You have to do your best to follow suit. Our defensive meeting room is right next to the Lombardi Trophies."

46. "Rocky, you won't be able to play again. It's impossible."

**Answers**

1. Green Bay Packers coach Vince Lombardi in 1970, two years before the Steelers made the playoffs.
2. Jack Lambert
3. Steelers announcer Myron Cope after Washington Redskins owner Daniel Snyder sent someone into the broadcast booth during a 2000 game to tell Cope to stop referring to his team as the "Wash Redfaces."
4. Greg Lloyd
5. Chuck Noll
6. Art Rooney, who was watching a preseason workout after reacquiring the franchise with Bert Bell and changing the nickname to Steelers in 1941.
7. Mike Tomlin
8. Joe Greene
9. John McKay
10. Chuck Noll, a year after winning the Super Bowl.
11. Levon Kirkland
12. Joe Greene
13. Houston Oilers coach Bum Phillips after losing to the Steelers in the playoffs 34–5.
14. Lee Flowers
15. Art Rooney
16. Bill Cowher
17. Terry Bradshaw

18. Jack Lambert
19. Ray Mansfield
20. Art Rooney
21. Ben Roethlisberger after Super Bowl XLV
22. Raiders coach John Madden, who claimed that the Steelers intentionally froze the sides of the field at Three Rivers for the 1974 AFC Championship game in order to slow down his wide receivers. The Steelers say that the tarp accidentally ripped overnight.
23. Jim Otto on facing Joe Greene
24. Ernie Holmes on Miami, the site of Super Bowl X.
25. Jack Lambert, after referee Ben Dreith ejected him for knocking out Browns quarterback Brian Sipe.
26. Denver rookie quarterback John Elway after Jack Lambert knocked him out of his first game as a pro in 1983.
27. Greg Lloyd
28. Hines Ward
29. Philadelphia Eagles owner Jeffrey Lurie
30. Jack Lambert
31. Troy Polamalu after Super Bowl XLV
32. Kevin Greene
33. Barry Foster
34. Mike Tomlin
35. Greg Lloyd after Joe Namath accused him of being a dirty player.
36. Bubby Brister after refusing to go in for Neil O'Donnell in 1991.
37. Neil O'Donnell
38. John McKay about Lynn Swann.
39. Orlando Brown
40. Mike Tomlin
41. Seattle coach Mike Holmgren
42. Chuck Noll during Franco Harris' holdout in 1984.
43. Mike Tomlin
44. Troy Polamalu
45. Larry Foote
46. Dr. John Baughman to Rocky Bleir in 1969.

## *Nine*

# Nearly 80 Years, Nearly 80 Questions

**Anniversaries can always be a tricky thing. Don't believe it? Try forgetting one and see what happens.**

When the Pittsburgh Steelers celebrated their fifth year in the National Football League in 1937, they went 4–7.

The 10th year they went 7–4, which was the first winning season in franchise history.

The franchise's "Silver Season" (25-year anniversary) wasn't exactly a memorable one either. The Steelers went 6–6 and had still only made the playoffs once up to that point.

It took another 15 years for Pittsburgh fans to celebrate a playoff win.

By the time the Steelers' 50th anniversary came around in 1982, the franchise was coming off arguably the most dominant decade in league history and had won four Super Bowls. So needless to say, the 50th anniversary all-time team had a number of new additions.

**Offense**: C Mike Webster; G Sam Davis; G Gerry Mullins; T Larry Brown; T Jon Kolb; TE Elbie Nickel; WR John Stallworth; WR Lynn Swann; RB Franco Harris; RB Rocky Bleier; QB Terry Bradshaw.

**Defense**: DL L.C. Greenwood; DL Dwight White; DL Joe Greene; DL Ernie Stautner; LB Andy Russell; LB Jack Lambert; LB Jack Ham; DB Mel Blount; DB Jack Butler; DB Mike Wagner; DB Donnie Shell; P Pat Brady; K Roy Gerela.

These questions are from specific years in Pittsburgh Steelers history.

Terry Bradshaw talks things over with Chuck Noll during a game in November 1978.
*(Getty Images)*

# Quiz!

1933: Who's considered the Steelers' first quarterback?

1937: Who was brought in to be the player/coach? (Bonus: Who was the player/assistant coach?)

1938: Who led the league in rushing?

1940: Who did Art Rooney sell the Pittsburgh franchise to and what team did he buy part interest in?

1941: What epic trade occurred that resulted in the franchise being renamed the Steelers?

1946: In what three major categories did Bill Dudley lead the NFL?

1950: What five other teams were allocated to the American Conference with Pittsburgh? (Bonus: Of them, name which one won the NFL championship.)

1952: What were the Steelers the last NFL team to abandon?

1953: Joe Bach, who stepped down at season's end due to health reasons, was part of what famous collegiate football group?

1958: Which future Hall of Fame quarterback was acquired in a trade with the Detroit Lions?

1962: True or false? During his final NFL season, Bobby Layne guided the Steelers back into the playoffs.

1965: Who quit two weeks before the season opener, saying "I can't work with this bunch of stiffs?" (Bonus: What happened the first time he quit just before the start of a season?)

1968: Although the Steelers finished 2–11–1, why was the tie important?

1970: Which two longstanding NFL teams moved with the Steelers into the newly created AFC?

1971: Who spiked the ball in celebration on the 3-yard line against Kansas City on *Monday Night Football*?

1974: Who led the Steelers in passing during the first Super Bowl season?

1975: How many consecutive wins did the Steelers have before losing the regular-season finale at the Los Angeles Rams?

1977: Who intercepted a pass and had a pass intercepted in the same game?

1979: What milestone did Chuck Noll achieve?

1980: True or false? Pittsburgh went from first place in the AFC Central to last.

1981: What injury against the Raiders may have signaled the end of the Steelers being a Super Bowl contender under Chuck Noll?

1982: What major change did Chuck Noll make to the defense?

1983: How old was Franco Harris when he had his final 1,000-yard season?

1987: Which replacement player during the strike went on to have a long career in the NFL?

1989: True or false? After losing the season opener 51–0 to Cleveland, and the following week 41–0 to Cincinnati, Pittsburgh came back to make the playoffs.

1991: Who announced his retirement at the end of the season?

1992: How many 100-yard games did Barry Foster have en route to a conference rushing title? (Bonus: Give the number of yards he finished with.)

1995: Which team did Pittsburgh beat to advance to its first Super Bowl in 16 years?

1996: Which three Steelers were named All-Pros?

1998: What controversial ending occurred during the Thanksgiving game at Detroit?

2000: Who spiked the ball before the play was over against Jacksonville?

2003: Why was Bill Cowher upset about playing a Monday night game at Cleveland?

2004: What was the only team to beat the Steelers in the regular season? (Bonus: Name the franchise-changing injury in that game.)

2005: What first did Pittsburgh pull off in the playoffs en route to winning "One for the Thumb?"

2007: Which franchise did the Steelers beat on the road for the first time, 41–24, on December 20?

2008: Which two players made up the Steelers' best sack combination since it became an official statistic in 1982?

2010: What prominent defensive team record did the Steelers set?

**Answers**

1933: Bernard "Tony" Holm

1937: Johnny "Blood" McNally was the player/coach, with Walt Kiesling a player/assistant coach.

1938: Rookie Byron "Whizzer" White

1940: Art Rooney sold the Pittsburgh franchise to Alexis Thompson and bought part interest in the Philadelphia Eagles.

1941: Art Rooney and Bert Bell traded the Philadelphia Eagles to Alexis Thompson for the Pittsburgh Pirates and then renamed the team the Steelers.

1946: Rushing, interceptions, and punt returns.

1950: The Cleveland Browns, New York Giants, Philadelphia Eagles, Chicago Cardinals, and Washington Redskins. The Browns won the league title.

1952: The single-wing for the T-formation.

1953: Joe Bach was one of Notre Dame's "Seven Mules," the linemen for the "Four Horsemen."

1958: Bobby Layne

1962: False, but he came pretty close. Passing for 1,686 yards Layne led Pittsburgh to a 9–5 second-place finish in the Eastern Conference. However, the New York Giants went 12–2 and subsequently lost to Green Bay in the NFL championship.

1965: Coach Buddy Parker. The last time he quit before the start of a season was with the 1957 Detroit Lions, who went on to win the NFL championship. This time he was right in as Pittsburgh went 2–12.

1968: Not only was it Pittsburgh's last tie before the overtime rule took effect, but the 28–28 stalemate against the St. Louis Cardinals ended up deciding the Century Division. Although the Cardinals swept their games with the Browns, Cleveland advanced to the playoffs with a 10–4 record while St. Louis was 9–4–1.

1970: The Baltimore Colts and Cleveland Browns.

1971: Wide receiver Dave Smith.

1974: Joe Gilliam

1975: 11

1977: Tony Dungy

1979: By returning for his 10th season, Chuck Noll became the longest tenured head coach in team history, surpassing Walt Kiesling.

1980: False, although the Steelers did finish third in the division and missed the playoffs.

1981: Terry Bradshaw sustained a broken hand and the Steelers lost their last two games without him to finish 8–8.

1982: After Joe Greene retired, Chuck Noll switched the defense to a 3–4 scheme.

1983: 33

1987: Quarterback Steve Bono.

1989: True. The Steelers finished 9–7 and then beat Houston 26–23 in overtime in a wild-card game before losing at Denver on a John Elway last-minute drive.

1991: Chuck Noll

1992: 12, which tied Eric Dickerson's league record, en route to 1,690 total yards.

1995: The Indianapolis Colts. They won 20–16.

1996: Jerome Bettis, Chad Brown and Dermontti Dawson.

1998: Jerome Bettis claimed he called the coin toss in overtime as tails, while referee Phil Luckett said he heard heads and awarded the ball to the Lions, who won 19–16.

2000: Plaxico Burress

2003: The Steelers were the only team that season to play on the road following a Monday night game. They lost at San Francisco the night the 49ers retired Ronnie Lott's No. 42, 30–14, but came back to beat the Browns for the first of 12 straight times, 13–6.

2004: The Baltimore Ravens, 30–13 in Week 2, when Tommy Maddox was lost for the season and Ben Roethlisberger took over at quarterback.

2005: Pittsburgh was the first team since the 1970 AFL–NFL merger to win a Super Bowl without playing a single home playoff game.

2007: The Steelers beat the St. Louis Rams, which had previously called Cleveland and Los Angeles home, for the first time on the road.

2008: James Harrison and LaMarr Woodley combined for 27½ sacks, with Harrison setting a franchise record with 16.

2010: The Steelers yielded just 62.8 rushing yards per game, beating the previous team record of 74.7 set in 2001.

*Ten*

# Draft/Trades

Since Chuck Noll was hired by the Steelers in 1969, the franchise has had a reputation for drafting well and finding the kinds of players that thrive in that setting. During a six-year period, Pittsburgh selected nine Hall of Famers—only missing in 1973—and wound up dominating the decade.

Obviously an interesting debate among Steelers fans can always be had about who was the best draft pick in franchise history. Joe Greene? Mel Blount? Jack Lambert? Terry Bradshaw? Troy Polamalu?

But if you really want to get him or her into a lather, make the discussion about who was the worst draft pick in franchise history.

Running back Dick Leftridge, a first-round pick in 1966, only lasted one season. Tackle Jamain Stephens, a first-round pick in 1996, showed up to training camp in 1999 so far out of shape that he collapsed while running a set of 40-yard-dashes, only to have Greg Lloyd stand over him and count him out like a boxer. Needless to say, he was cut. Arguments can be made for the likes Troy Edwards, John Reinstra, Tim Worley, and Deon Figures, however many consider the absolute worst to be Florida linebacker Huey

Richardson, the 15th overall pick in 1991 who lasted just five games before being released.

However, in his book *My 75 Years with the Pittsburgh Steelers and the NFL*, Dan Rooney made an interesting argument for Gary Glick, the only defensive back in history to be selected first overall in 1956.

"A few weeks earlier, [head coach Walt] Kiesling had gotten a letter from the coach at Colorado [State] in Fort Collins, telling us that he had a great player, a defensive back named Gary Glick. Kies was a big defensive guy and he decided we needed Glick more than anybody since Whizzer White." Rooney didn't see film on Glick until after he was drafted. "Our hearts sank," he said.

Glick lasted three seasons with the Steelers and bounced around the league until 1963. He played in 71 games and made 14 interceptions. Among those the Steelers passed on were Hall of Famers Lenny Moore, Forrest Gregg, and Sam Huff, as well as Pro Bowlers Earl Morrall, Joe Marconi, and Preston Carpenter.

1.  Who was the first player to be drafted by the franchise?
2.  Why did Hall of Fame defensive tackle Ernie Stautner last until the second round of the 1950 draft?
3.  Who did the Steelers select in the ninth round of the 1955 draft, only to cut him?
4.  Who did the Steelers pass on Jim Brown to select in the 1957 draft?
5.  Despite that, what quarterback did the Steelers trade for and what did the deal entail?
6.  How long was he with the Steelers?

7. What maneuvering in 1964 backfired on the Steelers?
8. When Pittsburgh took Joe Greene with the fourth-overall pick in the 1969 NFL Draft, who were the first three selections?
9. What was the front-page headline of the *Pittsburgh Post-Gazette* the next day?
10. Who was Pittsburgh's 10th-round pick in that draft?
11. In 1970, who did the Steelers trade for wide receiver Roy Jefferson?
12. With which team did Pittsburgh win a coin flip for the No. 1 selection in 1970 and who was the selection?
13. Who did it take in the third round?
14. How many future Hall of Famers did Pittsburgh take in the 1974 draft?
15. Name them.
16. What rounds were they selected?
17. What overall selection did Pittsburgh have in the first round that year?
18. Why did the NFL strip the Steelers of their third-round draft pick in 1979?
19. When the Steelers passed on Dan Marino in 1983, whom did they select?
20. Which quarterback was acquired from the Miami Dolphins for a third-round pick in 1984?
21. Which quarterback was acquired from the Kansas City Chiefs for a fourth-round pick in 1988? (Bonus: Name who he was related to on the team.)
22. Which team was Mark Malone traded to in 1988?
23. In 1993, to which team did the Steelers trade running back Tim Worley for two conditional draft picks?
24. In 1996, what did Pittsburgh give up to get running back Jerome Bettis from the Rams?
25. Which team did the Steelers trade Santonio Holmes to, and what did they get in exchange?
26. Who was reportedly on the trading block prior to the 2010 season due to off-field issues?

**Answers**

1. Notre Dame back Bill Shakespeare.
2. At 6'1" and 230 pounds, he was considered an undersized lineman.
3. Johnny Unitas
4. Len Dawson
5. Pittsburgh acquired Earl Morrall from San Francisco in addition to rookie lineman Mike Sandusky in exchange for two first-round draft picks, plus linebacker Marv Matuszak.
6. Earl Morrall was with the Steelers for one season before he was traded with two draft picks for Bobby Layne.
7. The Steelers selected Pitt standout Paul Martha and traded incumbent flanker Buddy Dial to Dallas for the draft rights to defensive lineman Scott Appleton, the Cowboys' first-round selection. However, Appleton, who had played with the Texas Longhorns, signed with the AFL Houston Oilers and Martha didn't pan out.
8. O.J. Simpson (Buffalo Bills), George Kunz (Atlanta Falcons), and Leroy Keyes (Philadelphia Eagles).
9. "Who's Joe Greene?"
10. L.C. Greenwood
11. Roy Jefferson was traded to the Baltimore Colts for Willie Richardson and a future draft choice.
12. The Chicago Bears. The Steelers selected Terry Bradshaw.
13. Mel Blount
14. Four, an NFL record.
15. Lynn Swann, Jack Lambert, John Stallworth, and Mike Webster.
16. Round 1: Lynn Swann; Round 2: Jack Lambert; Round 4: John Stallworth; Round 5: Mike Webster.
17. 21st
18. The team practiced with pads during offseason drills, which was against NFL rules.
19. Texas Tech defensive lineman Gabe Rivera.
20. David Woodley
21. Todd Blackledge. His father Ron was the Steelers' offensive line coach.
22. The San Diego Chargers.
23. The Chicago Bears.
24. A second-round pick and a future fourth-round selection.
25. Santonio Holmes, who was facing a four-game suspension at the start of the 2010 season and would be a free agent at the end of the year, went to the New York Jets for a fifth-round pick.
26. Ben Roethlisberger, with the supposed asking price of a top-10 pick in the draft.

# Eleven

# The Postseason

When your history is as rich and successful as the Pittsburgh Steelers, one rival just isn't enough. The Steelers are one of the few teams that can lay claim to having multiple tiers of rivals.

During the regular season it's mostly the division teams: the Baltimore Ravens, Cincinnati Bengals, and Cleveland Browns. Yet when you're constantly near the top of the division there's bound to be some other regular adversaries. In the playoffs, the Oakland Raiders used to be a frequent opponent, the team the Steelers had to get through to reach the AFC Championship Game or Super Bowl in the 1970s. Just mentioning the Immaculate Reception in downtown Oakland can still lead to a rough night. Fast-forward 20-some years and the New England Patriots were frequently in Pittsburgh's way.

As for the Super Bowl, the Steelers have faced the Dallas Cowboys three times—the most frequent matchup in the game's history. In an odd twist of fate, when Pittsburgh finally played the Green Bay Packers for the Lombardi Trophy the game was played in Cowboys Stadium.

Although the franchise dates back to 1933, Pittsburgh fans had to wait until 1947 to experience their first playoff game (a 21–0 loss to Philadelphia), and January 12, 1975 to play in their first championship, Super Bowl IX.

Since then the Steelers have for the most part made the most of their opportunities, with the most Lombardi Trophies (six), the most wins in the AFC Championship Game (eight) and the most home conference championship games (11).

1. Through the 2010 season, with which team were the Steelers tied for most postseason wins?
2. Which team had the most home playoff wins?
3. Who are the only two coaches to reach two Super Bowls during their first four seasons as head coach?
4. Who holds the NFL record for sacks in consecutive postseason games?
5. Who held the previous record?
6. How many Steelers have won the Heisman Trophy and also been named Super Bowl MVP?
7. Who was the last Steelers running back to post consecutive 100-yard rushing playoff games?
8. Which two receivers are tied for the team's postseason record for career 100-yard receiving games?
9. True or false? Pittsburgh recorded the only shutout in Super Bowl history.
10. Before Super Bowl XL, what was the NFC's record in Super Bowls shown on ABC?

11. Which Super Bowl that included the Steelers set the attendance record of 103,895?
12. True or false? Shortly before Super Bowl XXX it was discovered that some Internet proxy servers were blocking the game's official web site.

**Answers**

1. The Dallas Cowboys
2. The Steelers with 20, one more than the Dallas Cowboys and Oakland Raiders.
3. Mike Tomlin and Joe Gibbs
4. Linebacker LaMarr Woodley, with seven.
5. Jason Buck, with five.
6. None. The only players to win both are Roger Staubach, Jim Plunkett, Marcus Allen, and Desmond Howard.
7. Merril Hoge during the 1989 playoffs, at Houston on December 31, 1989, and at Denver on January 7, 1990.
8. Hines Ward and John Stallworth, with five.
9. False, there's never been a shutout in a Super Bowl.
10. 6–0
11. Super Bowl XIV.
12. True, and if you don't understand why ask your parents.

## Super Bowl IX: Pittsburgh 16, Minnesota 6

1. Super Bowl IX was the last pro game played in what stadium?
2. Where was it supposed to be played?
3. Which team was favored?
4. What was Minnesota's defense known as?
5. What color jerseys did the Vikings wear?
6. Which two backup players were inserted for injured defensive starters? (Bonus: Name the players they replaced.)
7. True or false? The Steelers defense led the league in fewest total yards and fewest passing yards allowed.
8. Which team had given up fewer points?
9. True or false? Joe Greene was named the NFL's Defensive Player of the year for the second-straight season?
10. Who recorded the first safety in Super Bowl history?
11. What was "Mean" Joe Greene the first to do in Super Bowl history?
12. What was Franco Harris to the first to do in Super Bowl history?
13. True or false? Franco Harris had more yards rushing than the entire Minnesota offense.
14. What was the score at halftime?
15. How did the Vikings score their only touchdown?
16. Who made the block?
17. Who made the hit to force a fumble from John Gilliam at the 5-yard line?
18. Who fumbled the other time Minnesota got to the 5?
19. Who fumbled the second-half kick return to set up a Pittsburgh touchdown?
20. Who made the interception to essentially seal the victory?

21. Roughly how many people watched on television the Steelers win their first Super Bowl?
22. Who sang the national anthem?
23. What was the theme of the halftime show?

**Answers**

1. Tulane Stadium in New Orleans.
2. The Louisiana Superdome, but construction of the dome wasn't finished.
3. The Steelers were favored by three points.
4. The Purple People Eaters.
5. Purple, as Minnesota was the home team. Pittsburgh wouldn't wear white again in a Super Bowl until Super Bowl XL.
6. Linebackers Ed Bradley and Loren Toews, who replaced Andy Russell and Jack Lambert.
7. True, 3,074 total yards and 1,466 passing yards.
8. Pittsburgh had allowed 189, and Minnesota 195.
9. False, but he won it for the second time in three years.
10. Dwight White when he tackled Fran Tarkenton in the end zone.
11. Green was the first player to record an interception, forced fumble, and fumble recovery in a Super Bowl.
12. Harris was the first African-American and Italian-American to be named Super Bowl MVP.
13. True. Harris had 158 rushing yards while the Vikings had 119 yards of total offense.
14. 2–0
15. A blocked punt recovered by Terry Brown.
16. Matt Blair
17. Safety Glen Edwards. The popped right into the arms of Mel Blount for an interception.
18. Chuck Foreman, with the fumble forced by Joe Greene.
19. Bill Brown
20. Mike Wagner
21. 78 million
22. No one. It was performed by the Grambling State University Band, but backed by a Mardi Gras choir.
23. Tribute to Duke Ellington.

## Super Bowl X: Pittsburgh 21, Dallas 17

1. True or false, Super Bowl X was the first game played on AstroTurf at the Orange Bowl.
2. Which team was favored?
3. What was the nickname of the Cowboys' defense?
4. Of Pittsburgh's 11 defensive starters, how many were named to the Pro Bowl? (Bonus: Name them.)
5. The emergence of which two players led to better passing numbers for Terry Bradshaw?
6. Who led the Cowboys in interceptions during the regular season?
7. Which quarterback, Terry Bradshaw or Roger Staubach, had more passing yards during the regular season? (Bonus: Who had more touchdown passes?)
8. Which quarterback had more passing yards in the game? (Bonus: Who had more touchdown passes and who had more passes intercepted?)
9. What injury in a conference championship game nearly had a major impact on Super Bowl X?
10. Who said of him, "I'm not going to hurt anyone intentionally. But getting hit again while he's running a pass route must be in the back of [his] mind. I know it would be in the back of my mind."
11. Who was named MVP of Super Bowl X?
12. True or false? Terry Bradshaw never saw the game-winning touchdown because after throwing the ball he was hit in the head and knocked out of the game.
13. Who was covering Lynn Swann on his acrobatic 53-yard reception?
14. What happened on the first snap of the game, to foreshadow the game's outcome?
15. How many times was Roger Staubach sacked and who led the Steelers in that category?

16. After Steelers punter Bobby Walden fumbled the snap, who caught a touchdown pass on the very next play to open the scoring?
17. Who blocked the punt for a safety to spark the Steelers?
18. Who made the interception in the end zone as time expired?
19. True or false? The CBS telecast was viewed by 80 million people, the largest television audience to that point.
20. What was the overall theme of the Super Bowl?
21. Which group performed during halftime? (Bonus: What was the name of the halftime show?)
22. Scenes for what movie were filmed during Super Bowl X?

Lynn Swann making one of the most famous—and acrobatic—catches in NFL history.
*(Getty Images)*

**Answers**

1. False. It was the last game played on AstroTurf at the Orange Bowl. It had been installed in 1970, but replaced with grass after Super Bowl X.
2. The Steelers were favored by seven points.
3. The Doomsday Defense.
4. Eight: Defensive linemen Joe Greene and L.C. Greenwood; linebackers Jack Ham, Jack Lambert, and Andy Russell; and defensive backs Mel Blount, Glen Edwards, and Mike Wagner. Green was named to the Pro Bowl despite missing six games due to an injury.
5. Wide receivers Lynn Swann and John Stallworth. Both saw little playing time the previous season.
6. Linebacker Lee Roy Jordan led the team with six interceptions.
7. Roger Staubach had passed for 2,666 yards and 17 touchdowns, while Terry Bradshaw threw for 2,055 yards and 18 touchdowns.
8. Terry Bradshaw completed 9 of 19 pass attempts for 209 yards and two touchdowns with no interceptions, while Roger Staubach was 15-for-24 for 204 yards with two touchdowns and three interceptions.
9. Lynn Swann had sustained a severe concussion in the AFC Championship Game against the Raiders and spent two days in a hospital.
10. Safety Cliff Harris
11. Lynn Swann caught four passes for a record 161 yards, including the game-winning 64-yard touchdown pass in the fourth quarter.
12. True. Larry Cole made the hit and Terry Bradshaw didn't know what happened until after he had been helped to the locker room.
13. Cornerback Mark Washington.
14. L.C. Greenwood sacked Roger Staubach to force a fumble (that Dallas recovered).
15. Seven, with L.C. Greenwood notching three.
16. Drew Pearson
17. Steelers running back Reggie Harrison.
18. Pittsburgh safety Glen Edwards.
19. True
20. United States Bicentennial.
21. Up With People ("200 Years and Just a Baby: A Tribute to America's Bicentennial")
22. *Black Sunday*

## Super Bowl XIII: Pittsburgh 35, Dallas 31

1. True or false? Super Bowl XIII was the first rematch of a previous Super Bowl.

2. Which team was favored?

3. How many points did Pittsburgh give up in its two AFC playoff games?

4. What starter went on to become a Super Bowl–winning head coach?

5. True or false? Dallas became the first team to appear in five Super Bowls.

6. Besides the Lombardi Trophy, what distinction was at stake during Super Bowl XIII?

7. How many players from Super Bowl XIII wound up being enshrined in the Pro Football Hall of Fame? (Bonus: Name them.)

8. How many non-players from Super Bowl XIII wound up being enshrined in the Pro Football Hall of Fame? (Bonus: Name them.)

9. After playing his entire career with which organization did the Cowboys lure tight end Jackie Smith out of retirement?

10. True or false? Because they were the home team, the Cowboys had to wear their blue jerseys in Super Bowl XIII.

11. Who said before the game that "Terry Bradshaw couldn't spell cat if you spotted him the C and the A?"

12. True or false? Terry Bradshaw's 318 passing yards and four touchdowns were both Super Bowl records.

13. True or false? Terry Bradshaw was the first player since the AFL-NFL merger to be named both Super Bowl MVP and the Associated Press MVP during the same season.

14. True or false? Terry Bradshaw had the league's best passer rating in 1978.

15. True or false? The Cowboys were the first defending champion to lose in the Super Bowl.

16. True or false? The Cowboys are the only team in Super Bowl history to score 30 points or more in a Super Bowl and still lose.

17. Since Super Bowl XIII, how many times has the title game featured two quarterbacks with two Super Bowl victories apiece?

18. Who recovered the onside kick to set up Dallas' final touchdown?

19. Who had the heartbreaking drop in the end zone that combined with the extra point could have tied the game?

20. Which referee threw the controversial flag on Benny Barnes for pass interference?

21. Who recovered the onside kick to allow Pittsburgh to run out the clock?

22. What did NBC show before Super Bowl XIII?

23. Who did Terry Bradshaw tie for the longest pass in Super Bowl history, 75 yards?

24. Which quarterback had more passing attempts and completions?

**Answers**

1. True, the teams played in Super Bowl X.
2. The Steelers were favored by 3½.
3. 15
4. Tony Dungy
5. True
6. The victorious team would be the first three-time Super Bowl winner.
7. 14. From Pittsburgh: Terry Bradshaw, Franco Harris, Lynn Swann, John Stallworth, Mike Webster, Joe Greene, Jack Lambert, Jack Ham, and Mel Blount. From Dallas: Roger Staubach, Tony Dorsett, Randy White, Rayfield Wright, and Jackie Smith.
8. Six. From Pittsburgh: coach Chuck Noll and owners Art Rooney Sr. and Dan Rooney. From Dallas: Coach Tom Landry, general manager/president Tex Schramm, and defensive coordinator Ernie Stautner, who was a Hall of Fame defensive tackle for the Steelers.
9. The Cardinals
10. False. After losing Super Bowl V in their blue jerseys, the Cowboys persuaded the NFL to change the rule so the "home" team could choose to wear their dark or white jerseys.
11. Linebacker Thomas "Hollywood" Henderson.
12. True
13. True
14. False. It was Roger Staubach.
15. True
16. True
17. Zero
18. Dennis Thurman
19. Jackie Smith
20. Fred Swearingen
21. Rocky Bleier
22. NBC preceded the game with the network premiere of *Black Sunday,* the 1977 movie that depicted a terrorist attack and used footage shot during Super Bowl X between the two teams.
23. Johnny Unitas
24. Although Terry Bradshaw had a lot more yards than Roger Staubach, they both had the same number of pass attempts (30) and completions (17).

## Super Bowl XIV: Pittsburgh 31, Los Angeles Rams 19

1. Where was Super Bowl XIV played?
2. Which team was favored?
3. How man rushing yards did the Steelers give up to Larry Csonka and Earl Campbell in the AFC playoffs?
4. How many touchdowns did the Rams score in the NFC Championship Game?
5. True or false? This was the first Super Bowl to feature two pre-expansion teams.
6. True or false? The Rams are the only team with nine wins or fewer during the regular season to reach the Super Bowl.
7. Did the Rams score more points than their opponents?
8. What unusual distinction did backup quarterback Vince Ferragamo "achieve" while leading the Rams to wins in six of their last seven games?
9. True or false? Even though the game wasn't played in the Rams' home stadium, they were the first host team to reach the Super Bowl.
10. True or false? The Steelers set an NFL record by averaging 391 yards per game during the regular season.
11. True or false? Pittsburgh led the league in scoring with 412 points.
12. Which number was greater during the regular season: Terry Bradshaw's touchdowns or interceptions?
13. Which number was greater during the game: Terry Bradshaw's touchdowns or interceptions?
14. Which team led at halftime?
15. Who said at halftime, "How can you mess up this way? Didn't we go over these things a dozen times? You guys are standing out there like statues."?
16. Which team led at the start of the fourth quarter?
17. How many times did the lead change hands?

18. Who scored on a 73-yard touchdown pass to give Pittsburgh the lead for good?
19. Who made the crucial interception with 5:24 remaining?
20. Who scored the final touchdown after a controversial pass-interference penalty? (Bonus: Name the player flagged.)
21. Who set a Super Bowl record with 162 yards on kick returns?
22. Who sang the national anthem?
23. Who made the coin toss?
24. True or false? The famous Coca-Cola commercial with "Mean" Joe Greene tossing his jersey to a boy debuted during the Super Bowl.
25. How many players had played for any other NFL teams?

The unforgettable gaze of Jack Lambert. *(Getty Images)*

## Answers

1. The Rose Bowl in Pasadena, California.
2. The Steelers by 10½ points.
3. They combined for 35 yards as Pittsburgh beat Miami 34–14 and Houston 27–13. Campbell had only 15 after leading the league with 1,697.
4. Zero. The Rams beat Tampa Bay 9–0 on three field goals.
5. True. It didn't happen again until Super Bowl XLI.
6. False, but it didn't happen again until the Arizona Cardinals reached Super Bowl XLIII.
7. Yes, but barely: 323–309.
8. He completed less than 50 percent of his passes and had twice as many interceptions (10) as touchdowns (five).
9. True
10. False. The 6,258 yards averaged 391 per game, but was 31 short of the record.
11. True
12. He had 26 touchdowns and 25 interceptions.
13. He had three interceptions and two touchdowns.
14. The Rams had a 13–10 lead.
15. Steelers assistant coach Wood Widerhofer.
16. The Rams had a 19–17 lead.
17. Seven
18. John Stallworth
19. Jack Lambert, on a pass intended for Ron Smith.
20. Franco Harris, on a 1-yard run after Pat Thomas was penalized in the end zone.
21. Larry Anderson
22. Cheryl Ladd
23. Art Rooney
24. False. It was shown during the game but had already debuted on October 1, 1979.
25. None

## Super Bowl XXX: Dallas 27, Pittsburgh 17

1.  Which team did Pittsburgh defeat in the AFC Championship Game?
2.  What controversial play helped the Steelers win the game?
3.  Where was Super Bowl XXX played?
4.  True or false? It was the last Super Bowl played in a collegiate setting.
5.  Which team was favored?
6.  Who coached the Cowboys?
7.  True or false? He became the first coach to win both a collegiate national championship and Super Bowl.
8.  How many touchdowns did Emmitt Smith score in the game?
9.  Emmitt Smith became just the fifth player to score a touchdown in three different Super Bowls. Name the previous four.
10. True or false? Emmitt Smith had a 100-yard rushing performance.
11. Which team gained more yards?
12. How many Neil O'Donnell passes did Dallas intercept?
13. Why was that so unusual?
14. True or false? Super Bowl XXX was the only Super Bowl in which Dallas didn't have a turnover.
15. Which unlikely player was named Super Bowl MVP?
16. With which team did he go on to sign a big free-agency contract?
17. Who was the "other" Dallas cornerback?
18. True or false? Dallas became the first team to win three Super Bowls in four years.
19. Which player became the first to win five Super Bowls?
20. Where was the presentation of the Lombardi Trophy made?
21. Who sang the national anthem?

22. Who had his helmet stolen after the game?

23. What was the theme of the halftime show and who headlined? (Bonus: How did the performer leave the stage?)

24. At the time, what was the only television program watched by more people in the United States than Super Bowl XXX?

**Answers**

1. The Indianapolis Colts, 20–16.
2. On Neil O'Donnell's 5-yard touchdown pass to Kordell Stewart in the second quarter, replays showed Stewart stepped out-of-bounds before making the catch.
3. Sun Devil Stadium in Tempe, Arizona.
4. True. The stadium is on the Arizona State campus.
5. Dallas was favored by 13¾ points.
6. Barry Switzer
7. False. Jimmy Johnson was the first. Barry Switzer won three national championships at Oklahoma (1974, 1975, and 1985).
8. Two
9. Lynn Swann, Franco Harris, Thurman Thomas, and Jerry Rice.
10. False. He finished with 49 rushing yards.
11. The Steelers outgained the Cowboys 310–254, 201–61 in the second half. Pittsburgh also had a significant edge in first downs, 25–15.
12. Three
13. Neil O'Donnell entered Super Bowl XXX as the NFL's career leader in fewest interceptions per pass attempt.
14. True
15. Cornerback Larry Brown, who made two interceptions that led to 14 points.
16. The Oakland Raiders
17. Deion Sanders
18. True
19. Charles Haley, who had won two with San Francisco (XXIII and XXIV) and two previously with Dallas (XXVII and XXVIII).
20. For the first time the Lombardi Trophy was awarded on the field and not in the locker room.
21. Vanessa Williams
22. Emmitt Smith. It was returned to him several weeks later.
23. "Take Me Higher" was a celebration of the game's 30-year anniversary and featured Diana Ross. She left the stage in a helicopter.
24. The final episode of *M*A*S*H*.

## Super Bowl XL: Pittsburgh 21, Seattle 10

1.  Where was the game played?
2.  True or false? It was that area's first Super Bowl.
3.  What was the game's slogan?
4.  Which team was favored?
5.  Who made the coin toss?
6.  True or false? It was the first Super Bowl played on FieldTurf.
7.  True or false? The Seattle Seahawks are the only team in Super Bowl history to have their the city/state and nickname painted in the end zone.
8.  True or false? The Seahawks were the first team to reach the Super Bowl without having to play a division champion in the playoffs.
9.  True or false? Pittsburgh was the first No. 6 seed in the NFL playoffs to beat the conference's top-three seeded teams on the road and then win the Super Bowl.
10. True or false? The Steelers were the first team to win the Super Bowl without playing a single home game in the playoffs.
11. Which Steelers player was the only player to have also played in Pittsburgh's last Super Bowl (XXX)? (Bonus: Name the coach who also played in that game.)
12. Despite leading the NFL with 50 team sacks, who was Seattle's only defensive player named to the Pro Bowl?
13. What color jerseys did the Steelers wear and why?
14. Who had an early touchdown nullified by a controversial pass-interference call?
15. How many passes did Ben Roethlisberger complete in the first quarter?
16. Who scored Pittsburgh's first touchdown?
17. Who was the first wide receiver to throw a touchdown pass in a Super Bowl?

18. Who had more rushing yards, Seattle's Shaun Alexander or Pittsburgh's Willie Parker?
19. What two distinctions did Ben Roethlisberger accomplish?
20. Thirty of the previous 34 Super Bowl MVPs were introduced during a pregame ceremony. Which four were not there?
21. How many passes did Hines Ward catch to be named MVP?
22. Which player did the Steelers have lead them out for their introduction because he was playing before his hometown crowd?
23. Which name player retired in the offseason?
24. Who ended up designing the Super Bowl XL ring, which included five football-shaped diamond settings to represent the Steelers' five Super Bowl victories?
25. Who played the halftime show?

The Bus rumbles over the Seahawks in Super Bowl XL. *(Getty Images)*

**Answers**

1. Ford Field in Detroit
2. False, the Pontiac Silverdome hosted Super Bowl XVI.
3. The Road to Forty
4. Steelers by 4.
5. New England Patriots quarterback Tom Brady, who was representing the previous Super Bowl MVPs.
6. True
7. False, the Seahawks were first, but the Arizona Cardinals did likewise.
8. True
9. True
10. False. Green Bay did so en route to winning Super Bowl I, as did Kansas City for Super Bowl IV.
11. Cornerback Willie Williams was on the last Super Bowl team, while defensive backs coach Darren Perry also started.
12. Rookie middle linebacker Lofa Tatupu.
13. The Steelers were the home team, but it was the third Super Bowl history to elect to wear white (the Cowboys and Redskins being the others). Coach Bill Cowher said it wasn't a home game since it was being played in Detroit and not Pittsburgh. It should be noted, though, that Cowher's team wore black in Super Bowl XXX in Arizona.
14. Seattle wide receiver Darrell Jackson.
15. One
16. Ben Roethlisberger
17. Antwaan Randle El, who played quarterback in college.
18. Shaun Alexander had 20 carries for 95 yards, while Willie Parker had 10 carries for 93 yards including a 75-yard touchdown.
19. At age 23 he became the youngest starting quarterback in league history to win the Super Bowl, and his 22.6 quarterback rating was the lowest ever for a Super Bowl–winning quarterback.
20. Terry Bradshaw, Joe Montana, Jake Scott, and the late Harvey Martin.
21. Five, but for 123 yards and a touchdown.
22. Jerome Bettis
23. Jerome Bettis
24. Dan Rooney, Jerome Bettis, and Ben Roethlisberger.
25. The Rolling Stones

## Super Bowl XLIII: Pittsburgh 27, Arizona 23

1. Where was the game played?
2. Which team was favored?
3. True or false? The Cardinals were seeking their first NFL title.
4. What job did Ken Whisenhunt have before joining the Cardinals as head coach?
5. Who also followed him to Arizona?
6. Which former Super Bowl MVP led Arizona's offense?
7. Against which team in the playoffs did Pittsburgh set an NFL record by holding the ball for 14:43 of the third quarter?
8. Which opponent did Pittsburgh create five turnovers against in the AFC Championship Game, while beating them for a third time that season?
9. True or false? When the Cardinals won the coin toss, it was the 12th-straight time the NFC team did so in the Super Bowl.
10. With 18 seconds remaining in the first half, who made an interception in the end zone and returned it 100 yards for the longest play in Super Bowl history?
11. How did Arizona score a safety?
12. Who caught two touchdown passes, the second for 63 yards, to give Arizona a 23–20 lead?
13. Who caught the game-winning touchdown pass in the corner of the end zone with 35 seconds remaining?
14. Who had four receptions for 71 yards on Pittsburgh's final scoring drive?
15. Who was named game MVP?
16. Who foiled Arizona's Hail Mary attempt with 18 seconds remaining? (Bonus: Name who ended up with the ball.)
17. Kurt Warner's 377 passing yards were the second-most in Super Bowl history. Who holds the record?

18. When Mike Tomlin became the youngest coach in NFL history to win a Super Bowl, how old was he?
19. Previously, who was the youngest coach to win a Super Bowl?
20. What Super Bowl rushing records did the teams combine to set?
21. What did Pittsburgh improve to while wearing white jerseys in the Super Bowl? (Bonus: Name how many games the winning streak of teams wearing white had reached.)
22. Because of tough economic times, what was the game nicknamed?
23. Up to how much did a 30-second ad cost?
24. Who presented the Vince Lombardi Trophy to his hometown team?
25. Who played the halftime show?

Santonio Holmes somehow manages to keep his feet in bounds while catching the decisive touchdown of Super Bowl XLIII. *(Getty Images)*

**Answers**

1. Raymond James Stadium in Tampa.
2. The Steelers were favored by seven points.
3. False. While the Cardinals had not won a Super Bowl, they had won a league title. The Cardinals last won it in 1947, the longest championship drought in the league.
4. Ken Whisenhunt was the Steelers' offensive coordinator in Super Bowl XL.
5. Steelers offensive coordinator Russ Grimm. He and Ken Whisenhunt were thought to be the frontrunners to replace Bill Cowher, but without waiting to see if the Steelers would promote him, Whisenhunt took the head coaching job with the Cardinals. After Pittsburgh hired Minnesota Vikings defensive coordinator Mike Tomlin, Grimm also left.
6. Quarterback Kurt Warner
7. The San Diego Chargers, who lost 35–24.
8. The Baltimore Ravens 23–14.
9. True
10. James Harrison
11. Center Justin Hartwig was called for holding in the end zone.
12. Larry Fitzgerald
13. Santonio Holmes
14. Santonio Holmes
15. Santonio Holmes, who caught nine passes for 131 yards and a touchdown.
16. Linebacker LaMarr Woodley forced a fumble while defensive end Brett Keisel recovered.
17. Kurt Warner's 414 yards in Super Bowl XLIII. He also had the third-best performance with 365 in Super Bowl XXXIV, and consequently eclipsed Joe Montana's 1,142 career Super Bowl record in four games.
18. Mike Tomlin was 36 years and 323 days old.
19. Bill Cowher, who was 38 years and 265 days old.
20. Fewest rushing attempts (38) and fewest rushing yards (91).
21. 3–0, while teams in white had won five straight games.
22. The Recession Bowl
23. $3 million
24. Joe Namath
25. Bruce Springsteen and the E Street Band

## Super Bowl XLV: Green Bay 31, Pittsburgh 25

1. Where was the game played?
2. Which team was favored?
3. Who botched the national anthem?
4. What was noticeably absent from the sideline?
5. How many of its previous 10 playoff games had Pittsburgh won?
6. Who was the only NFL quarterback to have a better career postseason winning percentage than Ben Roethlisberger's .833?
7. Who were the first five quarterbacks in NFL history to start three Super Bowls in their first seven seasons, with Ben Roethlisberger becoming the sixth?
8. Before the Packers, how many times had a No. 6 seed in the NFC playoffs advanced to the Super Bowl?
9. Which is the only AFC team to accomplish that?
10. Who was Pittsburgh's only Pro Bowl selection on offense?
11. In which category did Pittsburgh's defense lead the league: sacks, fewest points, or rushing yards allowed?
12. Who was named the NFL Defensive Player of the Year?
13. After President Barack Obama said he would attend the Super Bowl if the Chicago Bears won the NFC Championship game, who said in a postgame speech, "The President don't want to come watch us at the Super Bowl. Guess what? We're going to see him."?

14. What did the Packers do as part of their team meeting the night before the game?
15. Who scored the first touchdown of the game?
16. How many teams have come back to win a Super Bowl after having an interception returned for a touchdown?
17. Who did so for Green Bay?
18. Who caught a touchdown pass right before halftime to close Pittsburgh's deficit to 21–10?
19. Who was the game's leading rusher?
20. What was the only Super Bowl record set in the game? (Note: Tied records don't count.)
21. How many turnovers did the Packers have?
22. How many turnovers did the Steelers have?
23. How many times has the team that made more turnovers won the Super Bowl?
24. How many first downs by penalty did the teams combine to record?
25. How many different Packers scored in the postseason, to set an NFL playoff record?
26. Who did Aaron Rogers join to become just the second NFL quarterback with 1,000 yards passing and nine touchdown passes in one postseason?
27. Between Green Bay and Pittsburgh, which rank first and second, which team has the league's best all-time postseason winning percentage?
28. What off-field issue turned into a public relations nightmare?
29. How many NFL titles has Green Bay won?

**Answers**

1. Cowboys Stadium in Arlington, Texas
2. Packers by 2½
3. Christina Aguilera
4. Cheerleaders. The Steelers haven't had theirs since 1970, and Green Bay hasn't since 1988.
5. Nine
6. Bart Starr, who was 9–1 (.900).
7. Troy Aikman, Tom Brady, John Elway, Bob Griese, and Jim Kelly.
8. None; the Packers were the first.
9. The Steelers were the No. 6 seed before winning Super Bowl XL.
10. Center Maurkice Pouncey, who didn't play in the Super Bowl due to injury.
11. All three. The Steelers led the NFL in sacks (48), fewest points (14.5), and rushing yards (62.8) allowed per game.
12. Safety Troy Polamalu
13. Charles Woodson
14. They got fitted for their ring sizes.
15. Jordy Nelson
16. None; they're 0–11.
17. Nick Collins
18. Hines Ward
19. Rashard Mendenhall, with 64 rushing yards and a touchdown.
20. Fewest combined rushing attempts, with 36. The Packers had 13 and the Steelers 23.
21. None
22. Three
23. Three
24. Zero
25. 11 different Packers scored touchdowns in the playoffs. The previous mark of 10 was held by the 1940 Chicago Bears, 1985 New England Patriots, and 1992 Dallas Cowboys.
26. Kurt Warner, with 1,147 passing yards and 11 touchdowns in 2008. Rogers had a four-game total of 1,094 passing yards and nine touchdowns.
27. Green Bay tops the league at 29–16 (.644), with Pittsburgh 33–20 (.623) in the playoffs.
28. Roughly 400 people didn't have a seat.
29. 13, including four Super Bowl wins in five appearances.

*Twelve*

# Hall of Fame

In 1961, the decision was made to build the Pro Football Hall of Fame in Canton, Ohio, the birthplace of the American Professional Football Association in 1920, later renamed the National Football League.

Canton was also where Jim Thorpe, perhaps the first big-name athlete to play the game, started his professional career with the Canton Bulldogs in 1915.

Being enshrined is considered the highest honor that can be bestowed in the sport, as evidenced by that inaugural class in 1963: Sammy Baugh, Bert Bell, Joe Carr, Earl "Dutch" Clark, Harold "Red" Grange, George Halas, Mel Hein, Wilbur "Pete" Henry, Robert "Cal" Hubbard, Don Hutson, Earl "Curly" Lambeau, Tim Mara, George Preston Marshall, John "Blood" McNally, Bronko Nagurski, Ernie Nevers, and Thorpe.

Since then the building was expanded in 1971, 1978, and 1995, and renovated in 2003 and 2008. Today numerous people associated with the Pittsburgh Steelers are forever honored there.

# Quiz!

1. Put in order the Steelers contingency in the Pro Football Hall of Fame by induction, from first to most recent.
2. List the jersey numbers for each Hall of Fame player.
3. There are five other Hall of Fame Steelers who were primarily linked to other teams. Name them. (Bonus: Name the years they were inducted.)
4. Who joined them in 2010? (Hint: He was the active defensive coordinator.)

**Answers**

1. Art Rooney (1964), Bill Dudley (1966), Bobby Layne (1967), Ernie Stautner (1969), Joe Greene (1987), John Henry Johnson (1987), Jack Ham (1988), Mel Blount (1989), Terry Bradshaw (1989), Franco Harris (1990), Jack Lambert (1990), Chuck Noll (1993), Mike Webster (1997), Lynn Swann (2001), John Stallworth (2002), Rod Woodson (2009).

2. Mel Blount, 47; Bill Dudley, 12; Joe Greene, 75; Jack Ham, 59; Franco Harris, 32; John Henry Johnson, 35; Walt Kiesling, 35; Jack Lambert, 58; Bobby Layne, 22; John Stallworth, 82; Ernie Stautner, 70; Lynn Swann, 88; Mike Webster, 52; Rod Woodson, 26.

3. Bert Bell (1941–46); Len Dawson (1957–59); Robert "Cal" Hubbard (1936); Johnny "Blood" McNally (1934, 1937–38); Marion Motley (1955).

4. Dick LeBeau, who was considered one of the finest defensive backs in Detroit Lions history. From 1959–72 he had 62 interceptions for 762 yards and three touchdowns.

## Mel Blount

1. What's his full name?
2. Where was he born?
3. Name three other sports in which Blount excelled.
4. Where did he attend college?
5. True or false? After being drafted in 1970, Blount immediately won a starting job.
6. True or false? Early in his pro career Blount was used as a kick returner.
7. What amazing statistic was he credited with in 1972?
8. What type of play was his specialty?
9. What's known as the "Mel Blount Rule?"
10. True or false? Blount had an interception in each of his 14 seasons.
11. When he led the league in interceptions in 1975, how many did have?
12. What major award did he also earn that season?
13. True or false? Blount was named MVP of the 1976 Pro Bowl?
14. How may career interceptions did he have?
15. Blount's fumble recovery in the 1979 AFC Championship Game led to the winning touchdown against which team?
16. Which number was greater, career interceptions for a touchdown or career fumble returns for a touchdown?
17. Which number was greater: times Blount played in a Super Bowl or times he was named an All-Pro?
18. What league position did he hold after retiring as a player?
19. Blount is in the sports hall of fame of which two states?
20. The Mel Blount Youth Home, a shelter and Christian mission for victims of child abuse and neglect, was first opened in what city? (Bonus: Name where the second home opened.)

**Answers**

1. Melvin Cornell Blount
2. Vidalia, Georgia, on April 10, 1948.
3. Baseball, basketball, and track.
4. Southern University in Baton Rouge, Louisiana.
5. False. He didn't start until 1972.
6. True. He had 36 returns for 911 yards for a 24.3 average.
7. Blount didn't give up a single passing touchdown.
8. Bump-and-run coverage. He physically overpowered most receivers.
9. It's a rule regarding pass interference, and commonly explained during games as defensive back can't interfere with or hinder a receiver after five yards.
10. True
11. 11
12. Blount was named the NFL's most valuable defensive player.
13. True
14. 57 interceptions for 736 yards.
15. The Houston Oilers.
16. He did both twice.
17. Both were four.
18. Director of player relations, from 1983–90.
19. Georgia and Louisiana
20. The first home opened in his hometown of Vidalia, and the second home in Claysville, Pennsylvania, near Pittsburgh.

## Terry Bradshaw

1. What Is Terry Bradshaw's middle name?
2. What national record did he set in high school?
3. Where did he play football in college?
4. How many times was Bradshaw named an All-Pro?
5. Which number was greater: career touchdowns or career interceptions?
6. How many times did Bradshaw throw for 300 yards or more in a game?
7. In 1979, who did Bradshaw share the *Sports Illustrated* cover with as "Sportsmen of the Year"?
8. True or false? During the strike-shortened 1982 seasons, Bradshaw was in so much pain from an elbow injury sustained during training camp that he needed a cortisone shot before every game.
9. In what statistical category did he tie for the league lead that season?
10. True or false? Bradshaw won his last playoff game and passed for 325 yards.
11. True or false? Bradshaw's last pass attempt went for a touchdown.
12. Which winning percentage as a starter was better, regular season or playoffs?
13. For which teammate did he serve as presenter for induction into the Pro Football Hall of Fame?
14. Name the three Burt Reynolds movies in which Bradshaw appeared.
15. Which number is greater: times Bradshaw has been married, books authored and/or co-written, or albums recorded?
16. True or false? Bradshaw was the first NFL player to have a star on the Hollywood Walk of Fame.
17. What was Bradshaw diagnosed with after his NFL career ended?
18. In 2005 what NFL team did a group including Bradshaw show interest in purchasing?
19. In what sport was he part owner of a team?
20. What superstar in that sport shot a series of spoofs with Bradshaw the night before he died?

## Answers

1. Paxton
2. While at Woodlawn High School in Shreveport, Louisiana, Bradshaw set the national record for throwing the javelin, 245 feet.
3. Louisiana Tech
4. One
5. Bradshaw had 212 career touchdowns and 210 interceptions.
6. Seven, of which three were in the postseason and two in a Super Bowl.
7. Willie Stargell of the Pittsburgh Pirates.
8. True
9. Touchdown passes, with 17.
10. False. The yardage is correct, but the Steelers lost to San Diego 31–28.
11. True. It was a 10-yard completion against the New York Jets, but Bradshaw felt a pop in his elbow and never played again.
12. Bradshaw was 14–5 in the playoffs (.737) and 107–51 in the regular season (.677).
13. Mike Webster
14. *Hooper*, *The Cannonball Run*, and *Smokey and the Bandit II*.
15. Bradshaw has recorded six country/western and gospel albums, written or co-written five books, and been married three times.
16. True
17. Clinical depression
18. The New Orleans Saints
19. NASCAR
20. Dale Earnhardt Sr.

## Bill Dudley

1. On what day was Bill Dudley born?
2. Where did he play college football, starring as the school's first All-American?
3. What major award did he win in 1941?
4. What interrupted his professional career?
5. In what three statistical categories did Dudley lead the league in 1946?
6. What was that accomplishment called?
7. In what statistical category that the league no longer recognizes did Dudley also lead?
8. How many players had led the league in four distinctly different statistical categories before Dudley pulled it off?
9. True or false? Dudley is the only player in football history to be named MVP at the pro, college, and military service levels.
10. Why did Dudley leave the Steelers in 1946?
11. How much was his contract worth with the Detroit Lions?
12. What team honor did he receive all three seasons with the Lions?
13. What was the final team he played for?
14. During his final three seasons what did he lead his team in each year?
15. What epic play did he make against the Steelers on December 3, 1950?
16. Who had made the punt?
17. True or false? Dudley is the only player in NFL history with a rushing touchdown, touchdown reception, punt return for a touchdown, kickoff return for a touchdown, interception return for a touchdown, fumble return for a touchdown, and a touchdown pass.
18. In what three other ways did he score points?
19. Which career number was greater: rushing yards or punting yards?

20. Which career number was biggest: interceptions, touchdowns, or field goals?
21. Which state inducted him in its sports hall of fame?
22. Who does the Downtown Club of Richmond, Virginia, give the Bill Dudley Award to each year?

**Answers**

1. December 24, 1921
2. The University of Virginia
3. The Maxwell Award
4. After World War II he broke out he wanted to become a Navy pilot, and even attended the Army's flight school before being asked to join the Army's football team to boost morale.
5. Dudley led the league in rushing (604 yards), interceptions (10, returned for 242 yards), and punt returns (27 for 385 yards).
6. The triple crown
7. Lateral passing
8. Zero
9. True
10. He didn't get along with coach Jock Sutherland and was ready to quit football when Art Rooney traded him to the Detroit Lions.
11. It was a three-year guaranteed deal for $20,000.
12. Team captain (1947–49)
13. The Washington Redskins
14. Scoring
15. He ran to the sideline, reached out and with both feet in bounds, caught a 60-yard punt at the Redskins 4-yard line, and then returned it for a 96-yard touchdown.
16. Joe Geri
17. True
18. Dudley kicked point-after attempts and field goals, and had a touchdown via a lateral.
19. Dudley had 3,057 career rushing yards and 7,304 punting yards.
20. Dudley had 44 total touchdowns, 33 fields goals made, and 23 interceptions.
21. Virginia
22. The state's top college football player.

 **Quiz!**

## Joe Greene

1. Where was Charles Edward Greene born?
2. Where did he play college football?
3. True or false? He's the only person associated with his alma mater in the College Football Hall of Fame.
4. Where did Greene's nickname originate?
5. True or false? During Greene's 29 collegiate games his team went 23–5–1 and the defense gave up less than two rushing yards per attempt.
6. True or false? Greene was initially upset that the Steelers drafted him.
7. What number other than No. 75 did Greene briefly wear in 1969?
8. What NFL award did Greene win after his first season in 1969?
9. What was Pittsburgh's record that season?
10. Which legendary NFL tough guy did he spit in the face of and challenge to a fight during a game?
11. Which Cleveland Brown did he repeatedly kick in the groin when he was down on the ground?
12. What slogan did he come up with for the 1981 season, which became a rallying cry for the franchise?
13. When Greene retired after the 1981 season, who replaced him in the starting lineup?
14. Although sacks didn't become an official statistic until 1982, how many did Greene have?
15. Out of a possible 190 regular-season games during his career, how many games did he play?
16. To how many Pro Bowls was Greene named?
17. How many times was he named an All-Pro?
18. On what three teams did he serve as an assistant coach?

19. True or false? Greene is one of four people outside of the Rooney family to have Super Bowl rings from Pittsburgh's first six championship teams.

20. True or false? The famous Coca-Cola commercial in which Greene says, "Hey, kid, catch!" was done in one take.

**Answers**
1. Temple, Texas, on September 24, 1946.
2. North Texas State, now known as the University of North Texas.
3. False, Hayden Fry was the head coach from 1973–1978, before he went to Iowa.
4. North Texas State was known as the "Mean Green."
5. True
6. True, because Pittsburgh had such a long history of losing.
7. No. 72
8. NFL Rookie of the Year
9. 1–13
10. Dick Butkus of the Chicago Bears.
11. Bob McKay
12. "One for the Thumb in '81," which was later shortened to "One for the Thumb."
13. No one. The Steelers switched to a 3–4 alignment that required one nose tackle instead of two defensive tackles.
14. 78½
15. 181
16. 10
17. Five
18. The Pittsburgh Steelers, Miami Dolphins, and Arizona Cardinals.
19. True
20. False. It took several takes because after gulping down an entire bottle, he kept burping.

## Jack Ham

1. What is Jack Ham's real name?
2. Where was he born and raised?
3. What was the only team outside of his home state that Ham played for?
4. Where did Ham play college football?
5. True or false? Ham was the last player chosen for a scholarship in 1967.
6. How many losses did he experience in three years of starting?
7. What ultimate compliment did his college coach give him?
8. What school record did he set that wasn't matched until 1989?
9. What jersey number did Ham wear in college?
10. True or false? It took Ham three seasons to start for the Steelers.
11. Ham was said to be the fastest Steeler over what distance?
12. What exclusive club, based on career statistics, did Ham join?
13. Which career number was biggest: sacks, fumble recoveries, or interceptions?
14. To how many straight Pro Bowls was he named?
15. How many times was Ham named an All-Pro?
16. How many regular-season games did he miss during his career?
17. Despite that, which Super Bowl did Ham miss due to an ankle injury?
18. Who was the only player to be issued Ham's No. 59 since he retired in 1982?
19. Which was Ham inducted into first: the Pro Football Hall of Fame or the College Football Hall of Fame?
20. What form of media did Ham work in after his playing days ended?

**Answers**

1. Jack Raphael Ham Jr.
2. Johnstown, Pennsylvania
3. After attending Bishop McCort High School he sent a postgraduate season at Massanutten Military Academy in Woodstock, Virginia.
4. Penn State
5. True
6. Three, compared to 29 wins, including two 11–0 seasons.
7. Joe Paterno said of him, "Jack Ham will always be the consummate Penn Stater."
8. He blocked three punts in 1968.
9. No. 33
10. False, he won a starting job as a rookie and made three interceptions in the preseason finale.
11. The first 10 yards.
12. He was in the defensive 20/20 club with at least 20 career sacks and interceptions.
13. Ham had 25 sacks, 21 fumble recoveries, and 32 interceptions.
14. Eight
15. Six
16. Four
17. Super Bowl XIV
18. His No. 59 was reissued once, to Todd Seabaugh, in 1984.
19. Ham was inducted into the Pro Football Hall of Fame first, in 1988, and into the College Football Hall of Fame in 1990.
20. Radio

## Franco Harris

1. Where was Franco Harris born?
2. Why there?
3. Where did he attend high school?
4. Where did he play college football?
5. True or false? Harris is in the College Football Hall of Fame.
6. When Harris was selected with the 13th pick in the 1972 draft, who did many fans think the Steelers should have taken?
7. What business did the two start in 1990?
8. True or false? Harris rushed for more than 1,000 yards his rookie season.
9. True or false? Harris averaged more than 1,000 rushing yards each season of his career?
10. How many times did he rush for 100 yards in a game?
11. How many touchdowns did Harris score?
12. How many fumbles did he have?
13. True or false? Harris' Super Bowl career totals of 101 carries for 354 yards are records and his four career rushing touchdowns are the most in Super Bowl history.
14. True or false? In 19 playoff games, Harris had more than 1,500 rushing yards.
15. What prestigious award did Harris win in 1976?
16. How many times was Harris selected for the Pro Bowl?
17. How many times was he named an All-Pro?
18. True or false? Harris played his entire NFL career with the Steelers.
19. When he retired, how many rushing yards shy of Jim Brown's record was Harris?
20. Which political party's national convention did Harris attend as part of the Pennsylvania delegation? (Bonus: Name the city it was held and which presidential candidate he voted for.)

**Answers**

1. Franco Harris was born on March 7, 1950, in Fort Dix, New Jersey.
2. His father was in the military and served in World War II, while his mother was from Italy.
3. Rancocas Valley Regional High School in Mount Holly Township, New Jersey.
4. Penn State
5. False, he was primarily a blocker.
6. Harris' college teammate, running back Lydell Mitchell.
7. Super Bakery, which produced nutrition-oriented foods for schoolchildren and was renamed Super Foods in 2006.
8. True, he had 1,055 yards on 188 carries for a 5.6 average.
9. False, but he was close with 12,120 yards on 2,949 carries during his 13-year career.
10. 47
11. 100, 91 rushing and nine receiving.
12. 90, which worked out to one every 32.76 carries.
13. False, they're tied for the second-most.
14. True, he had 1,556 rushing yards and 17 touchdowns.
15. The Man of the Year Award, now known as the Walter Payton Man of the Year.
16. Nine
17. Seven
18. False, his final season was with the Seattle Seahawks.
19. 192
20. The Democratic Party. The convention was in Denver and he voted for Barack Obama.

## John Henry Johnson

1. Where was John Henry Johnson born?
2. Where did he initially play college?
3. Why did he leave?
4. Where did he finish his college career?
5. In what round of the 1953 draft was he selected by the Steelers?
6. Instead of the Steelers, with which team did he initially sign?
7. With which team did he make his NFL debut in 1954?
8. True or false? He led the league in rushing that season.
9. Johnson was in the "Million-Dollar Backfield" with which two future Hall of Fame players?
10. To which team was he traded in 1957?
11. In 1957, which team did he help defeat to win his only NFL title?
12. How many years after he was drafted did Johnson finally play for the Steelers?
13. How did he end up with the Steelers?
14. What was Johnson the first player to do in franchise history?
15. True or false? He only did that once.
16. Did Johnson finish his career with the Steelers?
17. When he retired in 1966, who were the only three players in NFL history with more rushing yards?
18. True or false? Johnson had more than 1,000 career receiving yards.
19. How many touchdowns did Johnson score?
20. What was Johnson diagnosed with after his career was over?

**Answers**

1. He was born in Waterproof, Louisiana, on November 24, 1929.
2. St. Mary's College in California.
3. The school discontinued the program.
4. Arizona State
5. Second
6. The Calgary Stampeders
7. The San Francisco 49ers
8. False, he was second in the league with 681 yards.
9. Hugh McElhenny and Y.A Tittle
10. The Detroit Lions
11. The Cleveland Browns, 59–14.
12. Seven
13. He was acquired in a trade.
14. Johnson was the first Steeler to have a 1,000-yard rushing season.
15. False, he reached 1,000 yards again in 1964.
16. No, his 13th and final season was with the Houston Oilers in the American Football League.
17. Only Jim Brown, Jim Taylor, and Joe Perry had more rushing yards than Johnson's 6,803.
18. True, he had 186 receptions for 1,478 yards.
19. 55
20. Dementia

## Walt Kiesling

1. When and where was Walt Kiesling born?
2. For which college was he an offensive and defensive lineman?
3. Which prominent school did he turn down?
4. What was the first NFL team he played for?
5. How many games did that team play in 1926?
6. How many were on the road?
7. What was the second NFL team he played for?
8. What was the last NFL team he played for?
9. What position did he play?
10. What was his nickname?
11. For which legendary unbeaten NFL team was he a starter?
12. How many times was he named All-NFL?
13. How many stints did he have as Pittsburgh's head coach?
14. With how many other NFL teams did Kiesling serve as a head coach?
15. For which other NFL team was he an assistant coach?
16. Who did he share coaching duties with in 1943?
17. Who did he share coaching duties with in 1944?
18. How many winning seasons did he have?
19. What was his career coaching record?
20. How many years was he a pro player, assistant coach, and NFL coach?
21. For what gaffe is Kiesling probably best remembered?

## Answers

1. May 27, 1903, in St. Paul, Minnesota
2. St. Thomas
3. Notre Dame
4. The Duluth Eskimos
5. 29
6. 28
7. Pottsville Maroons
8. The Pittsburgh Pirates in 1937–38. He also played for the Chicago Cardinals, Chicago Bears, and Green Bay Packers.
9. Two-way guard
10. Big Kies
11. The 1934 Chicago Bears.
12. Three
13. Three
14. Zero
15. The Green Bay Packers
16. Greasy Neale, the head coach of the Eagles, when Pittsburgh and Philadelphia merged teams for the 1943 season.
17. Phil Handler, the head coach of the Chicago Cardinals, when they merged with Pittsburgh for the 1944 season.
18. Two
19. 30–55–5
20. 34
21. Cutting Johnny Unitas.

## Jack Lambert

1. What is Jack Lambert's middle name?
2. Where was he born?
3. What position did he play in high school?
4. Where did he play college?
5. What position did he switch to?
6. Which future famous coach was a college teammate?
7. Why did he last until the second round of the 1974 draft?
8. Who did the Steelers take in the first round?
9. True or false? They were the first two future Hall of Fame players selected in that draft.
10. True or false? Lambert won the starting job at middle linebacker as a rookie.
11. Which injured player did he replace?
12. What award did he win that year?
13. What major award did he win in 1976?
14. Through his first 10 years how many tackles per season did Lambert average?
15. Which number is greater: career interceptions or official sacks?
16. How many games did he miss due to injuries during his first 10 seasons?
17. What injury sidelined him in 1984?
18. Who many times was he named an All-Pro?
19. What did Lambert supposedly tell the Steelers equipment manager to do with his No. 58 when he retired?
20. Why was he called Count Dracula in Cleats?

**Answers**

1. Harold
2. Mantua, Ohio, on July 8, 1952.
3. Quarterback
4. Kent State
5. Defensive end
6. Nick Saban
7. Most thought at 6'3½" and 204 pounds, he was too small to play linebacker at the NFL level.
8. Lynn Swann
9. False, one pick before Lambert the Oakland Raiders took Notre Dame tight end Dave Casper.
10. True
11. Henry Davis
12. NFL Defensive Rookie of the Year
13. NFL Defensive Player of the Year
14. 146
15. Lambert had 28 career interceptions and 23½ official sacks.
16. Six
17. A painful toe injury
18. Seven
19. Never give it out again.
20. Lambert's four upper front teeth were knocked out by an elbow while playing basketball in high school. He wore a removable partial denture, but took it out for games.

 **Quiz!**

## Chuck Noll

1. What's Chuck Noll's given name?
2. In what future rival city was he born?
3. Where did he attend college?
4. In what round was Noll selected in the 1953 draft?
5. By which team?
6. With which two teams was Noll an assistant coach?
7. As a defensive coordinator, what record did his unit set?
8. Noll is credited with being in whose coaching tree?
9. How did Noll's first Super Bowl turn out?
10. When Noll was named the 14th head coach of the Steelers, how many of his predecessors had enjoyed winning records?
11. Name them.
12. Who was the first player drafted by the Steelers with Noll has head coach?
13. How many future Pro Football Hall of Fame players did he draft?
14. True or false? Noll won his first game as head coach.
15. When did he win his second game?
16. Under Noll's direction, which team did Pittsburgh record its first playoff win against?
17. What was the second team?
18. How many career games did he win?
19. Who gave Noll his nickname, Emperor Chaz?
20. Where is Chuck Noll Field?
21. What is he the only coach in NFL history to do?
22. How many times in the 1970s was he named NFL Coach of the Year?
23. How many times did he win the award and when?

## Answers

1. Charles Henry Noll
2. Cleveland, on January 5, 1932.
3. Dayton
4. The 20th round, 239th overall.
5. The Cleveland Browns
6. The Los Angeles/San Diego Chargers (1960–65) and Baltimore Colts (1966–68).
7. The 1968 Colts set the NFL record for fewest points allowed (144).
8. Sid Gillman
9. After beating the Cleveland Browns 34–0 in the NFL championship, the Colts were upset by the New York Jets in Super Bowl III, 16–7.
10. Two
11. Raymond Parker was 51–48–6 from 1957–64, and Jock Sutherland was 13–10–1 from 1946–47.
12. "Mean" Joe Greene
13. Nine
14. True, the Steelers won their 1969 opener against Detroit 16–13.
15. Week 4 of the 1970 season, after 16 straight losses. Pittsburgh beat Buffalo, 23–10.
16. Pittsburgh beat Oakland in an AFC divisional playoff game 13–7 on December 23, 1972.
17. The Buffalo Bills 32–14, in 1974.
18. 209
19. Announcer Myron Cope
20. St. Vincent College in Latrobe, Pennsylvania, where the Steelers hold training camp.
21. He's the only coach to win four Super Bowls.
22. Zero
23. Just once, in 1989.

## Art Rooney

1. What year was Art Rooney born?
2. From what country were his parents immigrants?
3. How many brothers and sisters did he have?
4. What part of Pittsburgh did Rooney grow up and live in until the day he died?
5. True or false? Rooney turned down numerous scholarship offers from Knute Rockne at Notre Dame.
6. In what sport was he named to the U.S. Olympic team?
7. In what sport did have a promising career until sustaining an arm injury?
8. True or false? Rooney played in the league that evolved into the NFL.
9. Which college did he graduate from?
10. What other three colleges did he attend?
11. When Rooney founded the franchise, how many current NFL teams were in existence at that time?
12. Why did Rooney name the franchise the Pirates?
13. What position with the franchise did Rooney have after World War II?
14. What did the Steelers become known as until the 1970s?
15. How many years did it take Rooney to win his first championship/Super Bowl?
16. After the 1974 season, who took over the day-to-day operations of the franchise?
17. True or false? Rooney would almost always use a late-round draft pick on a local player even if he had little chance of making the team.
18. When Rooney died in 1988, how did the Steelers honor him throughout the entire season?
19. True or false? A statue of Rooney sits at the former location of Forbes Field.
20. Where is Art Rooney Field?

## Answers

1. Rooney was born January 27, 1901, in Coulterville, Pennsylvania.
2. Ireland
3. Eight. He was the oldest.
4. Old Allegheny, now known as the North Side.
5. True
6. Boxing. He held middleweight and welterweight titles from the AAU Boxing Championships.
7. Baseball
8. False
9. Duquesne University
10. Indiana Normal School (now Indiana University of Pennsylvania), Georgetown University, and Washington & Jefferson College.
11. Six: The Boston Redskins (now Washington), Chicago Cardinals (now Arizona), Chicago Bears, Green Bay Packers, New York Giants, and Portsmouth Spartans (now Detroit Lions).
12. He had been a fan of the baseball team.
13. President
14. The lovable losers
15. The 42$^{nd}$ season was the charm.
16. Rooney's son Dan
17. True
18. The players wore a patch on their left shoulder with Rooney's initials, AJR.
19. False, it's outside of Heinz Field.
20. Duquesne University

## Dan Rooney

1. On what day was Daniel M. Rooney born?
2. True or false? When Art Rooney founded the franchise he said it was a gift to his son.
3. True or false? Dan Rooney never played football.
4. Who beat him out for the city's All-Catholic Team in 1949?
5. Where did he attend college?
6. What was his major?
7. What was Rooney's first position with the Steelers, in 1960?
8. What two components to the financial well-being of the NFL was Rooney a key part of?
9. What design plan of Three Rivers Stadium did he argue against?
10. Who followed Rooney as team president and was just the third person to hold the position?
11. Who else was in the Class of 2000 for the Pro Football Hall of Fame?
12. Instead of a position, what designation was Rooney given during his induction?
13. True or false? Rooney and his father, Art, are the only father-son combination in the Pro Football Hall of Fame.
14. At Rooney's direction, if you draw a straight line between the goalposts at either end of Heinz Field and extend it south, where will you eventually reach?
15. What's in the opposite direction?
16. With few luxury items, what's considered Rooney's guilty pleasure?
17. To what position was Rooney named in 2009?
18. Who named him to that position?
19. Is Rooney a registered Republican or Democrat?
20. What honorary title has he held since 2008?

**Answers**

1. July 20, 1932
2. True
3. False. He was a terrific quarterback for North Catholic High School.
4. Johnny Unitas. Rooney was the second-team selection.
5. Duquesne University
6. Accounting
7. Director of personnel
8. Rooney helped negotiate the collective bargaining agreement to end the strike of 1982 and was an architect of the salary cap.
9. Rooney wanted a dual-purpose stadium design instead of a horseshoe shape that would have favored baseball.
10. Art Rooney II
11. Howie Long, Ronnie Lott, Joe Montana, and Davie Wilcox
12. Contributor
13. False. They were the second. The first was the late New York Giants owner Wellington Mara and his father, Tim.
14. The fountain at the Point, where the three rivers (Allegheny, Monongahela, and Ohio) meet.
15. Rooney's house.
16. Flying. He would pilot his own plane to training camp and meetings.
17. United States ambassador to Ireland
18. President Barack Obama
19. Republican
20. Commander of the British Empire

## John Stallworth

1. Where was John Lee Stallworth born?
2. Despite that, where did he attend college?
3. What was his major?
4. In which conference was he named an all-conference player in 1972 and 1973?
5. True or false? Stallworth earned a starting job his rookie season.
6. In how many consecutive playoff games did he have a reception?
7. In how many consecutive playoff games did he score a touchdown?
8. What Super Bowl career record does Stallworth have?
9. True or false? Stallworth missed roughly one out of every five games during his career due to injuries.
10. In what year did he lead the AFC in receiving yards?
11. What award did Stallworth win in 1984?
12. Who had more career catches, receiving yards, and touchdowns: Stallworth or Lynn Swann?
13. Who are the only Steelers to have more career touchdowns?
14. How many 1,000-yard receiving seasons did Stallworth have?
15. How many rushing touchdowns did Stallworth have?
16. How many Pro Bowls did Stallworth play in?
17. True or false? Stallworth was never named an All-Pro.
18. How many times was he named team MVP?
19. What company did he start in 1986?
20. Which sports franchise did he become a part-owner in 2009?

**Answers**

1. Tuscaloosa, Alabama
2. Alabama A&M (Tuscaloosa is the home of the University of Alabama.)
3. Business administration with an MBA concentrating in finance.
4. All-Southern Intercollegiate Athletic Conference
5. False, he started his second season.
6. 17
7. Eight
8. Average yards per catch, 24.4.
9. True. He played in 165 games, but missed 44 due to a variety of injuries.
10. 1984, he had a career-high 1,395 yards on 80 receptions.
11. NFL Comeback Player of the Year
12. Stallworth, with 537 catches, 8,723 yards, and 63 touchdowns.
13. Franco Harris (100), Hones Ward (84), and Jerome Bettis (80)
14. Three
15. One
16. Four
17. False, he was named an All-Pro in 1979.
18. Two
19. Madison Research Corporation (MRC), which specialized in providing engineering and information technology services to government and commercial clients. It was sold to Wireless Facilities Inc.
20. The Pittsburgh Steelers

## Ernie Stautner

1. What's Ernie Stautner's full name?
2. Where was he born?
3. How old was he when his family left for the United States?
4. What did he do before attending college?
5. Where did he attend college?
6. What was his major?
7. True or false? Stautner is in the College Football Hall of Fame.
8. True or false? Stautner spent his entire playing career with the Steelers.
9. During his 14-year career, how many games did he miss?
10. How many times was he named to the Pro Bowl?
11. True or false? He was named an All-Pro more times than he was to the Pro Bowl.
12. How many safeties did he record?
13. When he retired, Stautner was third on the NFL's career list in what statistic?
14. How many Super Bowls did he win?
15. With which franchise did he begin his coaching career as an assistant?
16. With which team did he coach against the Steelers in the Super Bowl?
17. For which two other NFL teams was he an assistant coach?
18. Which team did he coach in the Arena League?
19. Why did he return to Europe in 1995?
20. When did Stautner win his final championship?

## Answer

1. Ernest Alfred Stautner
2. Prienzing-by-Cham, Germany
3. Three
4. He served in the United States Marine Corps
5. Boston College
6. Psychology
7. False
8. True
9. Six, but he frequently played with injuries including broken ribs, shoulders, hands, and nose.
10. Nine
11. True, Stautner was named an All-Pro 10 times.
12. Three, which was the NFL record when he retired.
13. Fumble recoveries, with 23.
14. Two: Super Bowls VI and XII.
15. The Pittsburgh Steelers
16. The Dallas Cowboys
17. The Washington Redskins (1965) and Denver Broncos (1991–93).
18. The Dallas Texans
19. To coach the Frankfurt Galaxy.
20. He led the Galaxy to the World Bowl in 1995 and 1996, winning in 1995.

## Lynn Swann

1.  Where was Lynn Curtis Swann born on March 7, 1952?
2.  When he was two years old, where did his family move?
3.  True or false? Swann first ran a 9.8 in the 100-meter dash in college.
4.  Where was Swann an All-American receiver?
5.  What did he get a degree in?
6.  Who said of Swann, "We ask Lynn to do many things, and he excels in all."
7.  What franchise record did he set as a rookie?
8.  What statistical category did he lead the league in his second season, 1975?
9.  True or false? He exceeded that number later on in his career.
10. How many receptions did Swann have in Super Bowl IX?
11. Despite that, how many receiving yards did he have in four Super Bowls?
12. What award did he win in 1981?
13. What did Swann do the following year?
14. How many seasons did Swann play?
15. How many times did he play all 16 games in a season?
16. How many 1,000-yard receiving seasons did he have?
17. Which number is greater: number of yards during Swann's best receiving season or career punt-return yards?
18. How many receiving touchdowns did he have?
19. How many times was he named an All-Pro?
20. To what position was he appointed by President George W. Bush in 2002?
21. What job did Swann try to land in 2006?
22. What did he name his fundraising committee?

## Answers

1. Alcoa, Tennessee, near Knoxville
2. San Mateo, California, near San Francisco
3. False. He first did it in high school for Serra High School in Foster City, California.
4. University of Southern California
5. Public relations
6. John McKay
7. Swann's 577 punt-return yards set a franchise record and at the time were the fourth most in NFL history.
8. Touchdowns, with 11.
9. False, but he did match it in 1978.
10. Zero. Terry Bradshaw only completed nine passes.
11. 364, which when he retired was an NFL record.
12. NFL's Man of the Year for community service.
13. He retired and accepted a full-time job with ABC, for which he had already been working part-time.
14. Nine
15. Once, 1978.
16. Zero. His career best was 880 yards in 1978.
17. Receiving yards, with 880 in 1978. He had 739 career punt-return yards.
18. 51
19. Three
20. Swann was named the chairman of the President's Council on Physical Fitness and Sports.
21. He was the Republican nominee for Pennsylvania governor, but lost to incumbent Ed Rendell.
22. Team 88.

# Quiz!

## Mike Webster

1. Where was Michael Lewis Webster born?
2. Where did he play college football?
3. Who did he split time with during his first two seasons?
4. How many seasons did Webster play?
5. How many games did he miss during his first 16 seasons?
6. How many consecutive seasons did he play without missing game?
7. How many consecutive starts did he make?
8. What sidelined him?
9. How many Pro Bowls was he named to?
10. How many times was he named an All-Pro?
11. How many years was a Webster a team captain?
12. With which team did he finish his career?
13. What did he originally sign on for with that franchise?
14. True or false? When he retired in 1990, Webster was the last active player in the NFL to have played on all four of Pittsburgh's Super Bowl–winning teams.
15. Where is Mike Webster Stadium?
16. In which state's sports hall of fame is Webster enshrined?
17. What was Webster diagnosed with before his death?
18. How old was Webster when he died?
19. What was he diagnosed with after his death?
20. Why did Webster's estate sue the National Football League?

## Answers

1. Tomahawk, Wisconsin, on March 18, 1952.
2. Wisconsin
3. Veteran Ray Mansfield
4. 17
5. Four
6. 10
7. 150
8. A dislocated elbow
9. Nine
10. Nine
11. Nine
12. The Kansas City Chiefs
13. He joined the Chiefs to be an offensive line coach, but ended up playing two more seasons.
14. True
15. Rhinelander High School, his alma mater.
16. Wisconsin
17. Amnesia, dementia, and depression along with acute bone and muscle pain.
18. 50
19. Chronic traumatic encephalopathy, a neurodegenerative disease.
20. Webster's estate argued that he was disabled prior to his retirement and was owed $1.142 million in disability payments under the NFL's retirement plan. The courts agreed.

## Rod Woodson

1. Where was Roderick Kevin Woodson born on March 10, 1965?
2. Where did he play college football?
3. What was his other reason for going there?
4. True or false? In addition to defensive back and kick returner, Woodson played some offense in college.
5. How many individual school records did he set or tie in college?
6. In what other sport was Woodson a two-time All-American?
7. What did he get his degree in?
8. On November 22, 1987, who did Woodson pick off for his first career interception?
9. In 1988, who beat Woodson in the NFL's Fastest Man Contest?
10. What major award did Woodson land in 1993?
11. What accomplishment was he the first to pull off in 1995?
12. What position change did he successfully make later on in his career?
13. Which three teams did Woodson play for after the Steelers?
14. Which did he help win a Super Bowl?
15. For which was on the losing side in a Super Bowl?
16. How old was Woodson when he led the NFL in interceptions for the first time?
17. Whose pass did he pick off for his last interception, on November 16, 2003?
18. How many interceptions did Woodson make during his career?
19. What two NFL interceptions records did he set?
20. How many fumble recoveries did he make, a record for defensive players?
21. At what three positions was he named to the Pro Bowl?
22. How many Pro Bowls was he named to?
23. When Woodson didn't pass a physical in 2004, who replaced him at free safety for the Raiders?

Rod Woodson chases down Bears' quarterback Jim Harbaugh during a December 1992 game.

## Answers
1. Fort Wayne, Indiana
2. Purdue
3. Woodson wanted to pursue a degree in electrical engineering.
4. True, he was a running back and wide receiver too, and in his final collegiate game gained more than 150 rushing and receiving yards in addition to making 10 tackles and forcing a fumble against rival Indiana.
5. 13
6. Track, setting school records in both the 60- and 110-meter hurdles.
7. Criminal justice
8. Boomer Esiason
9. Darrell Green
10. NFL Defensive Player of the Year
11. He was the first NFL player to return from reconstructive knee surgery in the same season. He sustained the injury while trying to tackle Barry Sanders in the season opener and returned to play in Super Bowl XXX.
12. He successfully switched from cornerback to safety.
13. The San Francisco 49ers (1997), Baltimore Ravens (1998–2001), and the Oakland Raiders (2002–03).
14. The Ravens in Super Bowl XXXV.
15. The Raiders in Super Bowl XXXVII.
16. 37
17. Daunte Culpepper
18. 71
19. Career interception return yards (1,483) and interception returns for a touchdown (12).
20. 23
21. Cornerback, safety, and kick returner.
22. 11, a record for a defensive back.
23. Stuart Schweigert, who broke Woodson's career interception record at Purdue.

# Thirteen

# The Immaculate Reception

**NFL Films called it the greatest play of all time...and the most controversial.**

On December 23, 1972, the Pittsburgh Steelers were hosting the Oakland Raiders in an AFC divisional playoff game at Three Rivers Stadium, which would result in the first postseason win in franchise history. Although Pittsburgh failed to reach the Super Bowl, losing in the AFC Championship to the Miami Dolphins, the victory was considered to be a major turning point for the Steelers, who went on to secure four Vince Lombardi Trophies before the end of the decade.

Specifically, Terry Bradshaw's attempt to John "Frenchy" Fuqua was deflected when he collided with Raiders safety Jack Tatum, with Franco Harris snaring the ball inches above the turf, just before it hit the ground, and running for the game-winning touchdown and a 13–7 victory.

At least, that's the way it reads in the scoring summary.

1. Who had just scored with 1:17 remaining to give the Raiders the lead?
2. What was the line of scrimmage?
3. What down was it and how many yards did Pittsburgh need for the first down?
4. How much time was left on the clock?
5. How many timeouts did Pittsburgh have?
6. At that point, who had the longest reception on the possession?
7. Who had had broken up two of the previous three pass attempts?
8. What play did Chuck Noll call?
9. Who was the play designed to go to?
10. Who pressured Terry Bradshaw on the play, forcing him to get rid of the ball?
11. Who said, "At first, all that could go wrong with the play went wrong"?
12. Why was there such a controversy over whether John Fuqua and Jack Tatum touched the ball?
13. When was that rule changed?
14. What was fullback Franco Harris' initial assignment on the play?
15. Who was covering him out of the backfield?
16. Who did Franco Harris stiff-arm en route to the end zone?
17. Who did referee Fred Swearingen telephone from the sidelines?
18. What rumor did this start?
19. What was Raiders guard Gene Upshaw's theory on the phone call?
20. How long after the play did Fred Swearingen signal it was a touchdown?
21. How did fans react?
22. Who said, while calling the play, "Last chance for the Steelers. Bradshaw trying to get away. And his pass is ... broken up by Tatum. Picked off! Franco Harris has it! And he's over! Franco Harris grabbed the ball on the deflection! Five seconds to go! He grabbed it with five seconds to go and scored!"?
23. For which network?

24. Who said, "It turned out to be one of the great moments in football history. It was a mistake—I guess it was an honest mistake. Fuqua knows he hit it."?
25. Who later wrote, "No matter how many times I watch the films of the Immaculate Reception play, I never know for sure what happened."?
26. Who wrote that film taken by a local TV station showed, "No question about it—Bradshaw's pass struck Tatum squarely on his right shoulder."?
27. Who said, "Franco made that play because he never quit on the play. He kept running, he kept hustling. Good things happen to those who hustle."?
28. Who said, "I went from the depths of despair to the apex of ecstasy."?
29. Who didn't see the play because he was praying?
30. True or false? Jack Tatum said immediately after the game that the ball didn't hit him, but later admitted that even after watching the replay he couldn't tell.
31. Which Raider who was involved in the play maintained that the ball hit John Fuqua?
32. What did he also claim?
33. True or false? John Fuqua insists that the ball hit Jack Tatum first.
34. In 2004, what did John Fetkovich, an emeritus professor of physics at Carnegie Mellon University, conclude after analyzing the game football and conducting experiments?
35. Whose comments from years previous did it seem to confirm?
36. What was perfectly in the way of an NBC end zone camera, keeping it from getting a clear shot of whether Franco Harris made the catch before the ball hit the ground?
37. After that game, how many consecutive years did the Raiders and Steelers meet in the playoffs? (Bonus: Name which team had the better record in those games.)
38. When was the last time the Raiders and Steelers met in the playoffs? (Bonus: Name the winning team.)
39. Who came up with the name "Immaculate Reception?"

**Answers**

1. Kenny Stabler, on a 30-yard run.
2. Pittsburgh had the ball at its own 40-yard line.
3. Fourth down, ten yards
4. 22 seconds
5. None
6. John Fuqua for 11 yards with 53 seconds remaining.
7. Jack Tatum
8. 66 Circle Option
9. Rookie Barry Pearson
10. Tony Cline and Horace Jones
11. Terry Bradshaw
12. At the time, NFL rules stipulated that once an offensive player touched a pass he was the only offensive player eligible to make the reception, otherwise it's an illegal pass.
13. 1978
14. To block
15. Linebacker Phil Villapiano, who was subsequently blocked by tight end John McMakin.
16. Jimmy Warren
17. Officials supervisor Art McNally, who was in the press box.
18. That instant replay, which had yet to be adopted by the NFL, was used to make the call. It was denied by everyone involved.
19. That Swearingen called to see if there were enough police on hand to ensure the safety of the players.
20. 15 minutes
21. They rushed the field. It took 15 minutes to clear them before the extra-point kick could be attempted.
22. Curt Gowdy
23. NBC
24. Raiders owner Al Davis
25. Raiders coach John Madden
26. Steelers announcer Myron Cope
27. Steelers coach Chuck Noll
28. Steelers center Ray Mansfield
29. Steelers defensive end L.C. Greenwood
30. True
31. Phil Villapiano
32. That he was illegally blocked.
33. False. Supposedly he told late owner Art Rooney, but as of this writing he has only said publicly that he knows exactly what happened but won't tell.
34. That that the ball must have bounced off Tatum, who was running upfield, rather than Fuqua, who was running across and down the field.
35. Terry Bradshaw, who maintained that he didn't throw the ball hard enough for it to bounce that far off John Fuqua.
36. The goalpost.
37. Four. They split the games, 2–2.
38. 1983. The Raiders won 38–10 and went on to win the Super Bowl.
39. Michael Ord, who made the suggestion with Myron Cope first using it on the air.

# Fourteen

# Miscellaneous

From the stadiums to the Super Bowls to the Hall of Famers, just about every aspect of the Pittsburgh Steelers has been covered, right?

Hardly.

This section will test your knowledge of Steelers oddities and eccentricities. We'll look at the one-hit wonders, the great moments, and the forgotten stories of Steelers lore.

What is the Hines Ward rule? What is the Steelers' official fight song? How much were the Steelers paid to switch to the AFC in 1970? What television show used Super Bowl IX as a plotline for the episode that aired the night before the game?

From the T-formation to "Whizzer" White to broken jaws; Kordell Stewart, the Rooney Rule, Al Bundy, and *The Steeler and the Pittsburgh Kid*, this chapter revels in the absurd and unbelievable.

# Quiz!

1. Which Steelers player went on to become the first African-American assistant coach in the league?
2. Why did he leave the Steelers?
3. What also did he go on to do?
4. What is the Rooney rule?
5. When was it passed?
6. What rule is known as the Hines Ward rule?
7. Whose jaw did he break, leading to the rule?
8. Which player was with the Steelers the longest: Chad Brown, Kevin Greene, or Mike Merriweather?
9. Of the three, who had the most sacks?
10. Who missed the entire 1988 season due to a contract dispute?
11. After signing the biggest contract in league history, what happened to Byron "Whizzer" White on his first NFL play?
12. How many league rushing titles has Pittsburgh won since Bill Dudley in 1946?
13. Who coached the Steelers in 1935–36 only to return in 1952 and introduce them to the T-formation?
14. After he retired, what did Bobby Layne say was the biggest disappointment of his career?
15. Who said, [Bobby] Layne never lost a game...time just ran out on him."?
16. What two coaches in franchise history failed to record a single win?
17. Pittsburgh selected Terry Bradshaw with the No. 1 pick in the 1970 draft despite taking which Pennsylvania native in the second round of the 1969 draft?
18. During the 1–4 start in 1976, who made the vicious sack that knocked out Terry Bradshaw for two weeks?
19. What very unusual distinction did Franco Harris and Rocky Bleier achieve in 1976?

20. Who was surprisingly cut in the middle of his 1984 training camp holdout for a better contract?
21. True or false? Chuck Noll lost his final game coaching the Steelers.
22. From 1964 to 2006, Pittsburgh primarily had how many starting centers?
23. Name them.
24. What defensive scheme did Dick LeBeau devise while serving as Pittsburgh's defensive coordinator?
25. What nickname have his players called him?
26. What's the Steelers' official fight song?
27. What television show used Super Bowl IX as a plotline for the episode that aired the night before the game?
28. Which team won the game in the show?
29. In what prominent exhibition game did the Steelers participate in 1962?
30. Who won?
31. What's the only season the Steelers didn't wear black and gold?
32. How was Art Rooney known to sign letters?

Franco Harris takes the handoff and sprints through a mighty gash in the Oilers' defense.
*(Getty Images)*

33. Who starred in the 1981 television movie *The Steeler and the Pittsburgh Kid*, which was based off the famous Coca-Cola ad with Joe Greene and Franco Harris? (Hint: He had a much bigger movie come out within a year.)
34. Who had the second-best single-game rushing performance in team history?
35. Which Pittsburgh-born quarterback threw six touchdown passes against the Steelers on September 8, 1991?
36. Who failed to make the 1969 roster, but went on to play a television character named Al Bundy?
37. True or false? The Steelers have a winning record in overtime.
38. How much were the Steelers paid to switch to the AFC in 1970?
39. In terms of point differential, what's the worst loss in franchise history?
40. When he retired in 2005, who was the only quarterback in NFL history to have more rushing touchdowns than Kordell Stewart?
41. Which two Hall of Fame quarterbacks did David Woodley have the distinction of succeeding with the Dolphins and Steelers?
42. How many points did the Steelers allow during the final nine games of the 1976 season?
43. Who was Pittsburgh's lone Pro Bowl player in 1988?
44. In what sport did Bill Cowher's wife play at the professional level?
45. How many players were on all four Super Bowl teams in the 1970s?

**Answers**
1. Lowell Perry
2. To attend law school
3. He was also the first black manager of an automobile plant and color analyst for CBS.
4. Led by the efforts of Dan Rooney, the Rooney rule requires teams to interview minority candidates for head coaching positions.
5. 2003
6. It's illegal to make blindside block if it comes from the blocker's helmet, forearm, or shoulder and lands to the head or neck area of the defender.
7. Keith Rivers
8. Mike Merriweather was with the Steelers for six seasons, while Chad Brown was there for four and Kevin Greene three.
9. Kevin Greene had 35½ sacks, compared to 13 for Mike Merriweather and 30 by Chad Brown.
10. Mike Merriweather

11. He was so nervous that on the opening kickoff of the 1938 season the ball hit him in the eye. However, he went on to lead the league in rushing.
12. Zero
13. Joe Bach
14. Not winning a championship with the Steelers.
15. Doak Walker
16. Bert Bell was 0–5, and Aldo Donelli was 0–5, both in 1941.
17. Notre Dame quarterback Terry Hanratty.
18. Joe "Turkey" Jones of the Cleveland Browns.
19. They both had 1,000-yard rushing seasons.
20. Franco Harris
21. False, he won his last two games, against Cincinnati and Cleveland by the identical 17–10 score, but at 7–9 the Steelers missed the playoffs.
22. Four
23. Ray Mansfield, Mike Webster, Demontti Dawson, and Jeff Hartings.
24. The zone blitz
25. Coach Dad
26. There is none
27. *The Mary Tyler Moore Show*
28. The Vikings. The show was supposedly set in Minneapolis. At the end of the episode, Moore announced over the credits, "If the Pittsburgh Steelers win the actual Super Bowl tomorrow, we want to apologize to the Pittsburgh team and their fans for this purely fictional story, for on the other hand, they lose, remember, you heard it here first."
29. The Playoff Bowl between the two second-place teams.
30. The Detroit Lions
31. When the team merged with the Eagles for the 1943 season it wore green and white.
32. "Good wishes always to you and yours — Art Rooney."
33. Henry Thomas, whose next movie was *E.T.: the Extra-Terrestrial*.
34. The second-best rushing performance in team history was John Fuqua with 218 yards on December 20, 1970 at Philadelphia.
35. Jim Kelly, Don Beebe caught four of them.
36. Ed O'Neill, who starred in the show *Married . . . With Children*. He signed in 1969, but didn't make the final roster.
37. True. Through the 2010 season the Steelers are 18–14–2 in overtime.
38. $3 million
39. 51–0, against the Cleveland Browns during the 1989 home opener at Three Rivers Stadium.
40. Steve Young
41. Bob Griese and Terry Bradshaw, respectively.
42. 28 (an average of 3.11 points per game).
43. Offensive lineman Tunch Ilkin.
44. Kaye Cowher played professional basketball for the New York Stars of the Women's Pro Basketball League.
45. 22

# The Two-Minute Drill

**We'll ease you into this.**

What was so unusual about the Pittsburgh Steelers season opener in 2010?

When they won in overtime, 15–9, against the Atlanta Falcons, it extended the Steelers' winning streak on Kickoff Weekend to eight—the longest in the NFL—and set a franchise record.

Pittsburgh won in overtime the previous year as well, 13–10 over Tennessee. It also beat Houston 38–17 in 2008, Cleveland 34–7 in 2007, Miami 28–17 in 2006, Tennessee 34–7 in 2005, Oakland 24–21 in 2004, and Baltimore 34–15 in 2003.

The Steelers improved to 17–8 when opening at home since 1970, with the victory over Atlanta extending that winning streak to six, dating back to a 16–0 loss to Baltimore in the final season-opening game at Three Rivers Stadium in 2000.

After playing the Falcons for the first time in an opener, the victory improved Pittsburgh to 40–32–4 in season openers, the most wins among AFC teams.

That's a taste of what you'll find in this section.

When it comes to Pittsburgh Steelers trivia, these are some of the hardest of the hard—ones even the most die-hard fans will struggle with.

Ben Roethlisberger and Alan Faneca take it all in as they hold the Lombardi Trophy after defeating the Seattle Seahawks 21-10 in Super Bowl XL.

 **Quiz!**

1. How many different places have the Steelers held training camp?
2. Name them, in order.
3. Who were known as Big Mo and Little Mo?
4. Who was known as the Human Bowling Ball?
5. Who was known as Twinkle Toes?
6. Who was the last player to wear No. 12 before Terry Bradshaw?
7. Who was the first Pittsburgh quarterback to have a 400-yard passing game? (Bonus: Name the opponent.)

8. Who was the only Steeler other than Ernie Stautner to wear No. 70?
9. Which future Steelers defensive coordinator once kicked Terry Bradshaw in the head during a game?
10. In 2007, Pittsburgh wore throwback jerseys without what's called "TV numbers" on the shoulders and sleeves along with what two other teams?
11. On the Steelers' all-time roster, who is listed first alphabetically?
12. The sale of what player to Washington led to the Pirates being outscored 62–14 over their last five games of 1938?
13. Who were the three men to coach the team during 1941 season, the first with the Steelers nickname?
14. Which Sammy Baugh understudy was sold by the Washington Redskins to the Philadelphia-Pittsburgh team for the 1943 season?
15. During the 1944 season, what was the combined Cardinals/Steelers team known as?
16. Who was the best man at Art Rooney's wedding? (Hint: He frequently called him "that bullheaded Irishman.")
17. As previously mentioned, Joe Bach was one of the Seven Mules to block for the Four Horsemen at Notre Dame. Name the other six.
18. After he was cut by the Steelers, where did Johnny Unitas next play during the 1955 season?
19. Who were the only two Steelers to cross the picket line and play during the 1987 strike?
20. When did Pittsburgh play in Toronto for the first time?
21. What high school teammate was also a favorite target of Terry Bradshaw's in college?
22. Who caught Terry Bradshaw's final NFL pass?
23. What else was that game remembered for?
24. At what address can Terry Bradshaw's star on the Hollywood Walk of Fame be found?
25. Since the mid-1960s, how many Steelers offensive linemen have started the first game of their rookie season?
26. Name them.

27. Jack Ham is one of only nine NFL players to be in the defensive 20/20 club (at least 20 career sacks and interceptions). Name the other eight.

28. Who is the only player or coach from Kent State in the College Football Hall of Fame?

29. Who was the last player Pittsburgh selected in Chuck Noll's first draft in 1969?

30. Name the six NFL teams that never won at Three Rivers Stadium.

31. Who came up with the name "Steely McBeam" and why?

32. According to the World Geodetic System, what are the coordinates for Heinz Field?

33. What's the only year in the history of the Pro Bowl that the Steelers did not have a representative?

34. If you filled the oversized bottles atop the Heinz Field scoreboard with ketchup and then emptied them on the field, how thick would the ketchup be?

35. Who was the lone official to signal that the Immaculate Reception was a touchdown?

36. When they huddled, which official said he thought it wasn't a touchdown?

37. True or false? More than 25 Steelers also played in the USFL.

38. Name them and what teams they played for.

39. Name the offensive players on the Steelers' 75th Anniversary team.

40. Name the defensive players.

41. Name the two special-teams players.

42. Since 1969, the Steelers have named a team MVP. Name them in order.

4. Charley Tolar
5. Fran Rogel
6. Terry Nofsinger (1963–64).
7. Bobby Layne threw for 409 yards against the Chicago Cardinals on December 13, 1958.
8. Darwin Horn (1950).
9. Jim Haslett in 1979 while playing for the Buffalo Bills.
10. The Cleveland Browns and Philadelphia Eagles.
11. Running back Walter Abercrombie (1982–87).
12. Rookie Frankie Filchock, who still led the team in passing.
13. Bert Bell started the season as head coach, gave way to Buff Donelli, with Walt Kiesling back in charge by midseason. The team went 1–9–1, pulling off a 14–7 upset of the Brooklyn Dodgers (which came back to win a rematch 35–7).
14. Roy Zimmerman.
15. The Carpets, who went 0–10 and were 108–328.
16. Joe Bach
17. The Seven Mules were Bach, Chuck Collins, Ed Hunsinger, Noble Kizer, Rip Miller, Adam Walsh, and John Weibel.
18. The semi-pro Bloomington Rams.
19. Center Mike Webster and running back Earnest Jackson
20. In 1960 the Steelers played an exhibition against the Toronto Argonauts of the Canadian Football League and won 43–16 (despite playing under CFL rules). In 2008, the Steelers returned to Toronto to face the Buffalo Bills in the first game of the regular-season Toronto series.
21. Tommy Sprinks
22. Calvin Sweeney
23. It was the final NFL game played in New York City. The Jets moved to the Meadowlands in 1984.
24. 7080 Hollywood Blvd.
25. Three
26. Guard Tom Ricketts in 1989, tackle Marvel Smith in 2000 and center Maurkice Pouncey in 2010.
27. Joining Jack Ham in the 20/20 club are Ray Lewis, Seth Joyner, Donnie Edwards, Jack Lambert, Wilber Marshall, Williams Thomas, Ronde Barber, Brian Dawkins, and Rodney Harrison.
28. Don James, who coached at Kent State from 1971–74 with a 25–19–1 record, but is better known for his years at Washington.
29. Kent State kicker Bill Eppright
30. The Baltimore/Indianapolis Colts (0–11), Atlanta Falcons (0–5), New York Jets (0–4), Detroit Lions (0–4), Tampa Bay Buccaneers (0–2), and Carolina Panthers (0–1).
31. According to the Pittsburgh Post-Gazette, Diane Roles of Middlesex, Pennsylvania, submitted the winning name of "Steely McBeam," which was "meant to represent steel for Pittsburgh's industrial heritage, Mc for the Rooney family's Irish roots, and Beam for the steel beams produced in Pittsburgh, as well as for Jim Beam, her husband's favorite alcoholic beverage."

32. 40° 26' 48" N, 80° 0' 57" W
33. 1999
34. According to the Steelers' media guide, ¾ of an inch.
35. Back judge Adrian Burk.
36. No one did. Two officials said they thought it was a touchdown while three said they were not in a position to rule.
37. True
38. Anthony Anderson, Philadelphia Stars; Fred Anderson, Birmingham Stallions; Buddy Aydelette, Birmingham Stallions; John Banaszak, Michigan Panthers; Albert Bentley, Michigan Panthers; Fred Bohannon, Birmingham Stallions; Jackie Cline, Birmingham Stallions; Reggie Collier, Washington Federals; Charlie Davis, Houston Gamblers; Johnnie Dirden, Birmingham Stallions; Thom Dornbrook, Michigan Panthers; Glen Edwards, Tampa Bay Bandits; Dan Fike, Tampa Bay Bandits; Joe Gilliam, Washington Federals; Troy Johnson, Denver Gold; Tyrone McGriff, Michigan Panthers; Kelvin Middleton, Oklahoma Outlaws; Tom Moriarty, Michigan Panthers; Henry Odom, Orlando Renegades; Dave Opfar, Philadelphia Stars; Ray Pinney, Michigan Panthers; Rock Richmond, San Antonio Gunslingers; Lupe Sanchez, Arizona Wranglers; Jim Smith, Birmingham Stallions; Cliff Stoudt, Birmingham Stallions; Sydney Thornton, Oklahoma Outlaws; David Trout, Philadelphia Stars.
39. Jerome Bettis, RB (1996–05); Rocky Bleier, RB (1968, 1970–80); Terry Bradshaw, QB (1970–83); Larry Brown, OT (1971–84); Bennie Cunningham, TE (1976–85); Dermontti Dawson, C (1988–00); Alan Faneca, OG (1998—07); Franco Harris, RB (1972–83); Tunch Ilkin, OT (1980–92); Jon Kolb, OT (1969–81); Elbie Nickel, TE (1947–57); John Stallworth, WR (1974–87); Lynn Swann, WR (1974–82); Hines Ward, WR (1998–present); Mike Webster, C (1974–88)
40. Mel Blount, CB (1970–83); Jack Butler, DB (1951–59); Joe Greene, DT (1969–81); L.C. Greenwood, DE (1969–81); Jack Ham, LB (1971–82); Casey Hampton, NT (2001–present); Carnell Lake, S (1989–98); Jack Lambert, MLB (1974–84); Greg Lloyd, OLB (1988–97); Troy Polamalu, S (2003–present); Joey Porter, LB (1999–2006); Andy Russell, LB (1963, 1966–76); Donnie Shell, S (1974–87); Ernie Stautner, DT (1950–63); Dwight White, DE (1971–80); Rod Woodson, DB (1987–96)
41. Gary Anderson, K (1982–94) and Bobby Walden, P (1968–77)
42. 1969, Roy Jefferson; 1970, Joe Greene; 1971, Andy Russell; 1972, Franco Harris; 1973, Ron Shanklin; 1974, Glen Edwards; 1975, Mel Blount; 1976, Jack Lambert; 1977, Terry Bradshaw; 1978, Terry Bradshaw; 1979, John Stallworth; 1980, Donnie Shell; 1981, Jack Lambert; 1982, Dwayne Woodruff; 1983, Gary Anderson; 1984, John Stallworth; 1985, Louis Lipps; 1986, Bryan Hinkle; 1987, Mike Merriweather; 1988, Rod Woodson; 1989, Louis Lipps; 1990, Rod Woodson; 1991, Greg Lloyd; 1992, Barry Foster; 1993, Rod Woodson; 1994, Greg Lloyd; 1995, Neil O'Donnell; 1996, Jerome Bettis; 1997, Jerome Bettis; 1998, Levon Kirkland; 1999, Levon Kirkland; 2000, Jerome Bettis; 2001, Kordell Stewart; 2002, Joey Porter & Hines Ward; 2003, Hines Ward; 2004, James Farrior; 2005, Casey Hampton & Hines Ward; 2006, Willie Parker; 2007, James Harrison; 2008, James Harrison; 2009, Ben Roethlisberger; 2010, Troy Polamalu

# About the Author

Christopher Walsh has been an award-winning sportswriter since 1990, and currently covers the University of Alabama football program for BamaOnline.com. He's twice been nominated for a Pulitzer Prize, won three Football Writers Association of America awards, and received the 2006 Herby Kirby Memorial Award, the Alabama Sports Writers Association's highest honor. Originally from Minnesota and a graduate of the University of New Hampshire, he currently resides in Tuscaloosa, Alabama.

To make comments, suggestions or share an idea with the author, go to http://whosno1.blogspot.com/.

The author would like to thank Tom Bast for spearheading this project, and to everyone at Triumph Books who worked on it.